ARCO

Getting into Law School Today

3rd Edition

ARCO

Getting into Law School Today

3rd Edition

THOMAS H. MARTINSON, J.D.
and
DAVID P. WALDHERR, J.D.

Australia • Canada • Mexico • Singapore • Spain • United Kingdom • United States

THOMSON

ARCO

An ARCO Book

ARCO is a registered trademark of Thomson Learning, Inc., and is used herein under license by Peterson's.

About The Thomson Corporation and Peterson's

With revenues of US$7.2 billion, The Thomson Corporation (www.thomson.com) is a leading global provider of integrated information solutions for business, education, and professional customers. Its Learning businesses and brands (www.thomsonlearning.com) serve the needs of individuals, learning institutions, and corporations with products and services for both traditional and distributed learning.

Peterson's, part of The Thomson Corporation, is one of the nation's most respected providers of lifelong learning online resources, software, reference guides, and books. The Education Supersite[SM] at www.petersons.com—the Internet's most heavily traveled education resource—has searchable databases and interactive tools for contacting U.S.-accredited institutions and programs. In addition, Peterson's serves more than 105 million education consumers annually.

For more information, contact Peterson's, 2000 Lenox Drive, Lawrenceville, NJ 08648; 800-338-3282; or find us on the World Wide Web at www.petersons.com/about.

Third Edition

Library of Congress Number: 97-81129

ISBN: 0-02-862498-X

Printed in Canada

10 9 8 7 6 5   06 05 04

CONTENTS

PREFACE

- What are the top ten law schools in the country?
- How much weight do law schools give to the undergraduate GPA?
- When should I take the Law School Admission Test?
- Who should write my letters of recommendation?
- What should I say in my personal statement?

If you are planning to apply for admission to law school, these questions are of vital concern to you. This book provides answers to these and many other related questions.

For over fifteen years, we have been advising prospective law students on where to apply, how best to complete the application, how to prepare for the Law School Admission Test (LSAT), and similar issues. During this time, we have talked with tens of thousands of candidates and have reviewed countless applications. From this experience emerged the problems and issues that are addressed in this book. The advice we offer was also gleaned over many years and from many sources: interviews with law school deans, talks with college pre-law advisors, conferences and workshops on advising, and law fairs.

We are confident that the explanations and strategies offered in this book can help you ensure that your application will have the best possible chance for acceptance.

INTRODUCTION

The decision to become a lawyer is obviously one of the most important decisions you will ever make. For the immediate future, you are committing yourself to three years of rigorous academic study (four years in the case of part-time study), and you are making a large financial commitment—one that may leave you with a considerable debt burden when you graduate. (The total cost of a legal education at the nation's top schools can exceed $100,000.) Additionally, becoming a member of the bar is a career commitment that for most people lasts an entire lifetime.

Clearly, such an important decision involves many different factors and may be very difficult to make. The questions abound: Will I like school? What do lawyers do? Will I be successful? How will people regard me?, and so on. This book is NOT about such thoughts. Plenty of other books have been written about the law, law school, lawyers, and lawyering and may be useful in trying to decide whether or not to become a lawyer. This particular book is addressed to those people who have already decided to apply to law school. It is a "how to" book: how to get into law school.

Some people may think it peculiar for us to write a book giving instructions on how to fill out a law school application. They imagine that a law school application is, after all, nothing more than a series of simple questions about someone's personal history, questions that already have fixed answers that are entered into appropriate spaces on the application forms. To be sure, a law school application will contain some such questions. But the application process also poses problems that require serious thought for a solution, problems such as which of the 180-plus law schools to apply to, whom to approach for letters of recommendation, what to write in the personal statement.

The law school application process is not a simple one. Consider just the cost of applying to law school. The cost of registering to take the LSAT and for LSDAS (Law School Data Assembly Service) can easily exceed $300. The application fee charged by a law school can be as much as $65. So if you apply to several different schools, you will pay a few hundred dollars in application fees. The cost of an LSAT coaching course might be as much as $1,000. And you must also factor in the administrative costs associated with preparing the applications: costs for long-distance telephone calls, postage, and photocopying. This book will help you make sure that you get the most from the money you spend.

Furthermore, since decisions that you make about the content of the application have implications for your application's success or failure, these decisions have long-term implications for your career. It would be annoying indeed to learn that you have been rejected by your first-choice school because you chose the wrong person to write a letter of recommendation or because the content of the personal statement was inappropriate. This book will help you avoid making such errors.

As we noted above, this book is a "how to" book. Other publications address different issues. You will almost certainly want to acquire *The Official Guide to U.S. Law Schools,* published by Law Services (Box 2400, 661 Penn Street, Newtown, PA 18940-0977) or the *Official American Bar Association Guide to Approved Law Schools,* published by Macmillan Publishing USA. These guides provide valuable information about individual law schools and each guide is updated annually. Law School Admission Services also publishes *Financing Your Law School Education,* an invaluable guide on law school money matters.

Finally, this is a book for everyone applying to law school. The strategies we develop will help you create your best application regardless of the particular social or economic position you occupy. For those applicants with special concerns, we recommend *Looking at Law School* (Society of American Law Teachers, 1997: Meridian, ed. Stephen Gillers). That book contains chapters such as "Advice for Minority Students," "Issues of Special Concern to Women and Parents," and "Advice for Lesbians and Gay Men."

Getting into Law School Today

CHAPTER 1

THE STRUCTURE OF LEGAL EDUCATION IN THE UNITED STATES

Last year, approximately 45,000 new attorneys were admitted to the practice of law in the United States. With few exceptions, these newly licensed practitioners had successfully completed three years of full-time formal study (or the part-time equivalent thereof) at a professional school dedicated to the training of lawyers. In the United States today, it is all but impossible to become an attorney without first attending and graduating from a law school.

Although a formal law school education is now a prerequisite for admission to the bar, this was not always the case. During the colonial and immediate post-Revolutionary periods, law schools as we know them simply did not exist. The transmission of legal knowledge from one generation to the next depended primarily on an apprenticeship system under which law clerks learned the law while working in the offices of practicing attorneys.

Even today, while the law school seems preeminent, questions about legal education are not decided solely by the law schools themselves. Rather, the interests of the public, as represented by government, and the desires of the community of lawyers, as represented by various professional associations, also help to determine educational policies. The law school is just one star, albeit an important one, in a constellation that also includes a licensing/regulatory authority and a professional association. Our overview of the structure of legal education begins with the licensing authority.

LICENSING LAWYERS

In the United States, each state has its own procedures and rules for licensing those who wish to practice law within its borders. (The District of Columbia has a similar authority over its lawyers.) You cannot practice law in a state unless you have been admitted to that state's bar. ("Admitted to the bar" is another way of saying "licensed to practice law.")

Most states have three general requirements for admission to the bar:

1. You must have a law degree from a law school that is approved by the American Bar Association.

2. You must pass the state's qualifying exams for lawyers.

3. You must provide evidence of moral fitness and sound character.

There are very few exceptions to these rules, and we will remark on them below.

ABA APPROVAL

The American Bar Association, or ABA, is a national association for members of the legal profession. Its membership includes practicing lawyers, judges, law teachers, lawyers who are government officials or business executives, and even law students. The ABA sponsors a wide variety of activities and projects relating to legal ethics, legislation, and the practice of law. One of the most important of the ABA's functions is the accreditation of law schools.

Since the ABA is a professional association and not an arm of any government, the ABA lacks any real power to implement policy. It cannot discipline a lawyer or enact laws. But it can and does make recommendations to governmental authorities, and those recommendations are often adopted. Similarly, the ABA itself does not license or otherwise regulate law schools directly. It cannot officially order a law school to expand its library; it cannot force a law school to hire more faculty; it cannot require a law school to cease operation. But the ABA can achieve such results indirectly—through a state's rules regarding admission to the bar.

Virtually every state requires that a candidate for admission to the bar have a degree from a law school approved by the state. Some states actually go to the trouble of developing standards that a law school must satisfy and then determine whether those standards are met. Most, however, do not do so. Rather, the rules specify that "approved law school" means any law school "accredited by the American Bar Association." In effect, then, the ABA is the accrediting agency for law schools in the United States.

What happens to a school that fails to comply with the ABA's accreditation requirements? The ABA refuses to grant its approval to that school or withdraws its approval if one has already been granted. Without the ABA approval, the school won't appear on the list of approved schools of those states that defer to the ABA's judgment. As a consequence, graduates of the school are not eligible for admission to the bar in most states. And, as you can imagine, a school not on the ABA list is likely to have difficulty attracting applicants and students who are qualified for admission to other schools that are accredited by the ABA.

Obviously, then, you will want to attend an ABA-accredited law school. If you attend a law school that is not ABA approved, you will not be admitted to the practice of law. There are two exceptions to this rule: schools that are provisionally accredited by the ABA and schools that are not accredited by the ABA but are accredited by a particular state.

Law Schools Provisionally Accredited by the ABA

When a new law school begins operation, it does not automatically receive consideration for ABA approval. In fact, a law school must operate for at least one year before it is eligible to apply for ABA accreditation. Upon receipt of a request for approval, the ABA sends a team of investigators to the school making the request. If it finds that the school is in substantial compliance with the ABA's standards, then a provisional accreditation is issued.

During the provisional accreditation period, the ABA advises the school on what it needs to do to achieve full compliance with the ABA's accreditation standards. Once the school graduates its first class and is found to be in full compliance with ABA standards, then the school is added to the approved list. At that time, the new school's graduates are entitled to all the privileges of graduates of other approved schools.

What happens if the school fails to obtain accreditation in its third year? Then its graduates must wait until the school is able to secure ABA approval before they can claim the privileges enjoyed by graduates of approved schools. This means that those students must wait for admission to the practice of law in most states until such time as the school can obtain ABA certification. Once the full approval is obtained, it retroactively covers the school's other graduates. Obviously, attending a newly opened school or one only provisionally accredited by the ABA is a risky proposition. You may spend three years of your life studying to be a lawyer, pay substantial sums in tuition, and still not be able to practice law.

How can you evaluate the chances that such schools will eventually receive accreditation? The answer is "money." Virtually all of the requirements for ABA accreditation can be satisfied by spending money. If the school has the money to spend, it will receive accreditation. A new law school that is affiliated with an established university is a likely candidate for receiving ABA accreditation within a reasonable time.

One type of law school will never be eligible for ABA accreditation: the proprietary school. A proprietary school is run as a business to make a profit for its owners. Also included by the ABA in this category are institutions that are ostensibly not-for-profit but that pay organizers or directors exorbitant compensation. The ABA is adamantly opposed to educating lawyers at proprietary schools.

State Accredited Law Schools

A handful of states admit to the practice of law not only the graduates of ABA-approved law schools but also the graduates of law schools approved by a state-accrediting agency even when those schools are not approved by the ABA. While such schools do present an alternative to attending an ABA-approved school, there are serious disadvantages to the alternative.

First, since state-accredited schools fail to meet ABA accreditation standards, they generally do not provide a very good legal education. A 1979 report by the State Bar of California assessing the quality of education provided by non-ABA-accredited law schools in California concluded that the state-accredited schools "exploited applicants and students in various ways." In particular, the report noted the very poor record of the graduates of such schools in taking the California Bar Exam. In general, the pass rate of graduates of such schools was only about 10 percent.

Second, employment opportunities for graduates of state-accredited law schools are by and large limited to the accrediting state. A state that requires a degree from an ABA-approved law school as a condition of admission to its bar will not accept a degree earned from a law school approved only by a particular state. Thus, a graduate of a state-approved school who is successful in gaining admission to the bar of that particular state will not be eligible for admission in a state that requires a degree from an ABA-approved school.

THE BAR EXAM

In most states, even though graduation from an ABA-approved law school is a prerequisite for admission to the bar, the degree by itself does not automatically entitle its holder to be admitted to the practice of law. Candidates for admission to the bar must also take a comprehensive exam that tests their mastery of basic legal concepts and of the law of that state in particular. This battery is referred to as the *bar exam*.

As part of their licensing exam, many states use the Multi-State Bar Exam (MBE). The MBE is a standardized, multiple-choice test that can be used in any jurisdiction because it tests basic legal concepts as they might occur in the law of any state. Bar exams also rely heavily on essay questions that test the details of the law of the particular state. Increasingly, states also require a multiple-choice exam called the Multi-State Professional Responsibility Exam (MPRE). As the name implies, the MPRE is essentially an ethics exam.

THE LAW SCHOOLS

As of this writing, there are 175-plus ABA-accredited law schools. Although each law school is autonomous and adopts its own curriculum, course offerings across the nation are very similar. This similarity is not surprising, given that these schools all meet ABA standards and given that political, economic, and social issues are increasingly "national" issues.

The first-year curriculum at an ABA-accredited law school usually includes civil procedure, contracts, criminal law, property law, and torts, along with perhaps Constitutional law and almost surely a legal writing or methods course. The second year may include one or two requirements such as federal income tax and corporations. The rest of the course offerings are electives that fall into areas such as business transactions, civil procedure, environmental law, estates and trusts, family relations, health law, government regulation, individual rights, intellectual property, labor law, real estate law, taxation, and so on. Within these general headings, a school may offer several courses. For example, under the heading "Family Relations," you might find listed courses with the following names: Children and the Law, Adoption Clinic, Juveniles and the Justice System, and Matrimonial Practice.

The format within which the courses are presented is also fairly standardized. The full-time course of study usually requires three academic years, and students begin their studies in the fall and graduate in the spring about 33 months later. Even the exceptions to this rule are fairly standardized: part-time programs require four or perhaps five years; some schools allow for summer or winter admissions; some schools offer a semester abroad; law schools rarely accept transfer students, and so on.

This uniformity is not surprising, but the uniformity does not suggest that there are not significant differences among schools from the applicant's perspective. We do mean to say, however, that the differences between and among law schools must be assessed in the light of this uniformity. In Chapter 3, we discuss some important things to look for that will help you distinguish one ABA-accredited law school from another.

BAR REVIEW COURSES

Although the details of the law vary from state to state, it is not necessary to go to law school in the state in which you plan to practice. Indeed, a few states simply don't have a law school located within their boundaries. Furthermore, as noted above, a law school probably will not give very much emphasis to the law of the state in which it is located. Yale Law School, for example, which is located in New Haven, does not drill its students in the details of Connecticut procedure.

What, then, prepares a law student to take the bar exam? A bar review course. A bar review course is an intensive review of the basic legal concepts common to all jurisdictions and a crash course in the details of the law of a particular state. These courses are usually offered by private companies located in various states and are taught by law school professors and practicing attorneys. The courses last only a few weeks and are given before each bar exam.

ASSOCIATION OF AMERICAN LAW SCHOOLS

Most law schools accredited by the ABA are also members of the Association of American Law Schools (AALS), but this is not particularly important to you as a law school applicant. The AALS was formed at the suggestion of the ABA and held its first meeting in 1900. It was and still is concerned with the improvement of legal education from the point of view of the law school.

Because it is the ABA accreditation that determines whether you will be admitted to practice in most states, whether or not a school is a member of the AALS should not concern you greatly. As a matter of fact, most ABA-accredited law schools are also members of the AALS, and any difference in the quality of education offered by those that are and those that are not members can be explained in terms of other factors.

LAW SCHOOL ADMISSION COUNCIL/LAW SCHOOL ADMISSION SERVICES

The Law School Admission Council (LSAC) was founded in 1947 by some member law schools of the AALS, and its name may imply that its function is similar to that of the AALS. The mission of the LSAC, however, is much more specific than that of the AALS. Whereas the AALS is generally concerned with the improvement of law school education, the LSAC is specifically concerned with admissions practices. In fact, the LSAC was initially organized to oversee the creation of an admission test for law schools, and it continues to sponsor the Law School Admission Test (see below). The LSAC also provides other services to law schools and a variety of publications and services to prospective law school applicants. (See LSAT/LSDAS below.)

Law School Admissions Services (LSAS) is a nonprofit corporation that is the operating arm or, we could say, the business end of the LSAC. It exists to provide the services that the LSAC wants for its member schools. When you apply to law schools, you won't deal directly with the LSAC. Instead, you will contact LSAS:

Law Services
Box 2000
661 Penn Street
Newtown, PA 18940-0998
Telephone: (215) 968-1001

Additionally, Law Services operates the Candidate Referral Service that helps to match applicants (primarily members of minority categories) to law schools and Law Access, a program that helps applicants apply for educational loans. You can obtain information on these ser-
On-line: http:// www. lsac.org

vices by contacting Law Services:

Law Services
Minority Opportunities in Law
Box 40
661 Penn Street
Newtown, PA 18940-0040
(215) 968-1338

Law Access
Box 2500
661 Penn Street
Newtown, PA 18940-0900
(215) 968-7540

As a service to law school candidates, Law Services has written and distributes several publications that you will almost certainly find useful, including "The Right Law School for You," and "Financing Your Law School Education." You can order copies of these publications when you register for the LSAT and LSDAS. You can also order these publications by telephone (215-968-1314) or online (http://www.lsac.org).

LSAT/LSDAS

LSAT and LSDAS are acronyms for Law School Admission Test and Law School Data Assembly Service, respectively. These services are arranged for by LSAC and are provided by LSAS to assist law schools in processing applications and in making admissions decisions.

The Law School Admission Test is a multiple-choice, standardized exam that is given four times a year at many locations in the United States and Canada and in some important cities in other countries. Virtually all ABA-accredited and many non-ABA-accredited law schools require an LSAT score as part of the application process. In Chapter 6, we discuss the content of the LSAT in detail.

The Law School Data Assembly Service is, as the name implies, a service that summarizes important information about law school applicants. In addition to providing basic biographical background information about themselves, applicants must also arrange to have college transcripts forwarded to Law Services. Law Services then creates an LSDAS report summarizing this information and forwards copies of this report to the law schools designated by the applicants.

Because so much information must be provided to Law Services, the procedures for registering for the LSAT and LSDAS are complicated, but they are not difficult to understand. The details for registration along with the necessary forms are provided by Law Services in a 150-plus page "Information Book" that is updated annually. You can obtain a free copy of this registration guide by contacting Law Services at the address or telephone number given above.

PRE-LAW ADVISORS

Most colleges have one or more persons who are "pre-law advisors." These advisors may be members of the faculty who have agreed to take on the additional responsibility of advising pre-law students, or they may be full-time members of the career guidance office. Although pre-law advisors are not "officially" a part of the admissions process, they may be able to provide you with invaluable assistance.

Many advisors are members of the National Association of Pre-Law Advisors, the professional organization for pre-law advisors, and its regional counterparts. These associations sponsor regularly scheduled conferences at which the advisors attend workshops on various aspects of the law school application process and share information on advising with one another. An advisor who is a member of one or more of these organizations is likely to have a lot of good information about law schools and the application process. Even if you are no longer a college student, the pre-law advisor at your alma mater will probably be more than happy to chat with you about law school admissions and to give you access to any information the advisor's office has about law schools.

A good pre-law advisor will be able to help you make informed decisions about which schools to apply to and can help you develop an effective application. Additionally, your pre-law advisor may be the right person to ask for a letter of recommendation. Finally, some pre-law advisors may have direct contacts with certain schools. Although it is doubtful that a pre-law advisor can "pull strings" to get a student admitted if not otherwise qualified, a thoughtful recommendation from a pre-law advisor who is known to the school might, in a close case, tip the scales in favor of admission.

The great majority of pre-law advisors whom we have met are conscientious, hard-working, and knowledgeable professionals, and we have met many both on campus and at the conferences of their professional associations. Unfortunately, as is true of any profession, all practitioners are not created equal. Some give better advice than others, and a few give advice that we consider to be absolutely wrong.

One such piece of bad advice regards the need to take a preparation course for the LSAT. In particular, some advisors regard proprietary LSAT preparation courses as unnecessary or even as downright evil. From these advisors we hear remarks such as "My students are so good they don't need an LSAT preparation course" and "LSAT preparation courses are a waste of time and money." As unqualified statements, these remarks are certainly wrong.

The sentiment behind these remarks is understandable. Advisors tend to be protective of their students and so regard proprietary preparation courses with some skepticism, but categorical condemnations of such services do students a disservice. You may or may not need to take a preparation course, and in Chapter 6, we discuss the various ways of preparing for the LSAT. Our best advice is that you talk with other students who have taken a preparation course and ask their opinions of the value of such programs.

CHAPTER 2

THE ADMISSIONS PROCESS

In this chapter, we will examine the process that law schools use to decide which applications to accept and which to turn down. We understand that from your perspective as an applicant the admissions process may look like the proverbial "black box": applications are fed into the system and are ultimately discharged with an "admit" or "reject" stamped on them. The inner workings of the "black box," however, remain forever a mystery.

As an applicant, you want to know as much as possible about what will happen to your application *before* you pay the application fee. Unfortunately, you may not be satisfied by the descriptions typically given in the catalogues provided by law schools:

The committee considers all evidence that suggests academic and professional promise.

Candidates are evaluated on academic and personal criteria.

The committee considers each application on its merits.

These general descriptions are likely to leave you shaking your head and muttering to yourself, Yes, but what are they going to think of my application, my GPA, my LSAT score, my background?

Unfortunately, you cannot know in advance if you will definitely be accepted at a certain law school. Deciding whether or not a particular application ought to be approved is the function of the admissions process. Later in this chapter, we will describe how you can estimate your chances for success, but in the final analysis you have to pay your money and wait to see what happens.

WHAT REALLY HAPPENS

Although every law school has an admissions "black box," the "wiring" inside the box varies from school to school. At some schools, decisions are made by an admissions dean; at others, they are made by a faculty committee; and at still others, they are the responsibility of a professional administrator who is not a lawyer. And, of course, there are various combinations of these approaches.

We will describe for you the insides of the black boxes of four different law schools. Law schools are sensitive about their admissions decisions, so we cannot identify the schools described, and we have slightly changed the terminology used by the admissions officers to describe their procedures. Even so, these descriptions should give you a pretty good idea of what goes on inside the "black box" at most schools.

Our first school we will call "Rising Star Law School" because it is relatively young but building a nice reputation. At "Rising Star," applications are read by a pair of admissions officers who are themselves neither faculty members nor lawyers. Each application is read in its entirety by at least one administrator and sometimes by both administrators. The administrators then make a recommendation to accept, to reject, to waitlist, or to delay action on the application. The file along with the recommendation is forwarded to the Dean of Admissions. It is the Dean who is the actual seat of authority. The Dean then reviews the application in light of the recommendation and makes a final decision. In most cases, we were told, the Dean implements the recommendation of the administrator.

Our second school we will call "Ivy League Law School." Although this law school doesn't literally have any ivy on its building, its name always appears on any list of "top ten" law schools. At "Ivy," admissions decisions are made solely by the Dean of Admissions, who is a lawyer and a former member of the faculty. The Dean reads each and every application (including the letters of recommendation and the personal statement) and makes a final decision. During the busy season, the Dean may read over 200 applications in a single day.

Our third school we will call "Venerable Law School" because it has been around for quite a long time and enjoys a considerable reputation for academic excellence. At "Venerable," the admissions process is entirely "faculty driven." Admissions decisions are made by a committee of faculty members, and admission to this law school requires the near-unanimous consent of the committee. However, an application is not necessarily read by every member of the committee. Applications are initially sorted into two classes. Those that on the face appear to be very, very strong are assigned to category One. Those that on the face appear not to have a very good chance of acceptance are also assigned to category One. All other applications are assigned to category Two.

Notice that very strong and very weak applications are assigned to the same category. Why? Because a committee member's time is very valuable, it is just not feasible to have each application read by every member. Instead, applications are given to readers who have the authority to reject them or to refer them to the committee as a whole. Since category One applications are either very strong or very weak, they are given to only one reader. The theory is that the one reader will immediately see the merit in a strong application and refer it to the committee. As for the relatively weak applications, unless the one reader sees something extraordinary in the application, the application would not in any event receive the required number of votes for acceptance, so it would be rejected. Category Two applications–those in the middle–are read by two readers. If either reader detects something in the application that suggests the candidate should be accepted, then the application goes to the whole committee for debate. Having two readers minimizes the likelihood that an otherwise well-qualified applicant will be summarily rejected because a single reader did not fully appreciate the significance of some aspect of the application.

Finally, we will call our fourth school "Suburbia Law School" because it is located in the suburbs of a large city. "Suburbia" is a well-established school with a good academic reputation in its region. "Suburbia's" admissions process combines the "faculty driven" approach with the "Dean of Admissions" approach. Here, the Dean of Admissions, who is a lawyer and a member of the faculty, has the absolute authority to dispose of some applications by rejecting them and others by accepting them. For other applications, the Dean's authority is severely limited. These applications the Dean must forward to a committee of faculty members, which then makes the final decision.

At this school, administrative aids begin by sorting applications into one of three categories: A, B, or C. "A" is the strongest category, and "C" is the weakest. The Dean then reads every application. Applications in category "C" can be summarily rejected by the Dean. They cannot, however, be summarily accepted. If the Dean thinks that an application in the bottom tier should receive favorable action, then the Dean must forward the application to the faculty committee, which is free to act on or to ignore that recommendation. Applications in the highest category can be summarily accepted but not summarily rejected by the Dean. If the Dean thinks that, for some reason, a very strong application should be rejected, that application must be referred to the admissions committee. Finally, category "B" contains all the borderline applications. The Dean must refer all category "B" applications to the committee with a recommendation. The Dean has no authority to summarily dispose of a "B" or borderline application.

Although there are differences in the procedures used at the four schools, there are also some striking similarities. Two features in particular challenge attention. First, at each of the four schools, every application is read by someone. Applications are not routinely disposed of solely on the basis of the LSAT score and the GPA. Second, the amount of attention given to an application depends to a greater or lesser extent on the competitiveness of the application. And, as you might guess, competitiveness is largely a function of the LSAT score and the GPA. LSAT score and GPA largely determine how seriously an application is taken—as we will explain in the next section.

Indexing

Each year, law schools receive many more applications than the number of seats available in their entering classes. At some schools, the ratio of applications to available seats is three to one or four to one. Other schools may receive six or seven times more applications than they are able to accept. And at some schools the ratio of applications to available seats is an astounding twenty to one.

How do the admissions departments handle that kind of volume? Many schools presort applications according to likelihood of acceptance. In any given batch of applications are those that will almost certainly be accepted, those that will almost certainly be rejected, and those that could go either way. Obviously, relatively less scrutiny is needed for applications at the extremes.

One way of sorting applications is by using a number commonly called an index. The index is created by a mathematical formula that combines an applicant's LSAT score and undergraduate Grade Point Average. In fact, the scale used to score the LSAT was designed to facilitate indexing. LSAT scores range from 120 (the minimum) to 180 (the maximum). If the hundreds digit (the "1") is dropped, scores range from 20 to 80. If scores are then divided by 20, the results range from 1 to 4, and most undergraduate institutions grade on a similar scale. By manipulating LSAT scores in this way, the indexing formula can combine the GPA and the LSAT score weighing each about equally. In mathematical terms, the formula can be expressed:

$$\frac{\dfrac{(\text{LSAT} - 100)}{20} + \text{GPA}}{2} = \text{Index}$$

Let's take an example. We'll assume that an applicant has an LSAT score of 170 and a GPA of 3.4:

$$\frac{\dfrac{(170 - 100)}{20} + 3.4}{2} = \frac{\dfrac{70}{20} + 3.4}{2} = \frac{3.5 + 3.4}{2} = 3.45$$

This formula converts the 170 LSAT score to a 3.5 and then averages that number with the GPA. The beauty of this particular indexing formula is that it generates a number that has a range very much like the GPA. Thus, a 3.45 index looks like a B+, a 3.97 index looks like an A+, and a 2.85 index looks like a C+.

Of course, the index doesn't have to have any self-evident value. Equally possible is the following formula:

$$[(\text{GPA} \times 20) + 100] + \text{LSAT} = \text{Index}$$

Using the numbers above, we have:

$$[(3.4) \times 20) + 100] + 170 = [68 + 100] + 170 = 168 + 170 = 338$$

This formula generates a very artificial number, but that doesn't really matter so long as the person using the number understands what it means compared to other numbers. For example, a perfect LSAT score and a 4.0 GPA generate the top number of 360, and a median LSAT score of 150 and GPA of 3.2 combine to generate an index of 314. A law school admissions officer using such a formula will understand the different meanings of indexes such as 314 and 360.

Notice that the index is calculated using only a cumulative undergraduate GPA. Graduate school marks are not factored in. The index is an attempt to quantify the strength of an application according to a single, universal scale. Although a significant minority of applicants will have done graduate work, many more applicants will not have done any graduate work. Yet, excepting a few cases (applicants from foreign countries or from universities with nonstandard grading practices), every applicant will have a GPA. So the undergraduate GPA is used in the formula because of its universality. This is not to say, however, that graduate marks play no role in the admissions process. It is possible that an applicant's graduate school record would play a very important role—for good or for ill—in the assessment of that application. But graduate marks are not included in the index.

A formula may also include an adjustment for the "quality" of the candidate's undergraduate education. Quality is a reflection of both the reputation of the undergraduate institution and of the candidate's course selection and choice of major. At one of the schools described above, "quality" is actually a mathematical factor in the formula, but not in the way you might think. "Quality" is not interpreted in any subjective way, e.g., the general reputation of the school. Rather, "quality" is calculated on the basis of the performances of past law students who came out of that undergraduate institution. Thus, if over the years, students accepted from school X with a certain GPA and LSAT score have tended to do better at the law school than students from school Y with similar credentials, then applicants from school X will be given additional points over those from school Y.

At many schools, no mathematical adjustment is made to reflect "quality," but readers tend to make a mental adjustment of the index that reflects their subjective judgment regarding the quality of an undergraduate institution. This "fudge factor" is more or less valid but doesn't seem to be enormously important. An admissions dean with ten years of experience probably has a pretty good basis for distinguishing a 3.5 at one school from a 3.5 at another school. A reader with less experience has less reason to make the adjustment. In any event, there is nothing you can do about this tendency. If you are confident that your school is known for rigorous standards, you can upgrade your chances slightly when deciding to what schools to apply. On the other hand, if you have reason to believe that your undergraduate program was less demanding, make sure that you keep your expectations realistic.

Finally, a mental adjustment may also be made to take account of the era to which your GPA belongs. Law school admissions officers are well aware of the upward creep of grades over the past years and take this "grade inflation" into account in interpreting an applicant's index. Again, this is a matter that you cannot control. But if you have been out of school for some time, you can rest assured that readers will give you mental "bonus" points for the fact that your GPA was earned at a time when good grades were harder to come by.

You are now in a position to understand how the index works in conjunction with the structure of the admissions process at the schools we described above. At "Venerable Law School" and "Suburbia Law School," the index determines the routing of the application. At "Venerable," applications with very high and very low indexes are sorted in Category One and are read by one member of the admissions committee. All other applications are sorted into Category Two and are read by two members of the committee. Similarly, at "Suburbia Law

School," the index determines whether an application is an "A" application, a "B" application, or a "C" application.

At "Ivy," the Dean reads through every application. As the Dean reads the listing of activities, the employment history, the personal statement, and the letters of recommendation, the Dean is trying to "get a picture" of the candidate. Then the Dean forms a tentative judgment as to what action should be taken. Next the Dean consults the index. If the index confirms the Dean's impression of the candidate, then that action is made official. For example, if the "picture" of the candidate is very positive and the index is very high, then the application is approved. On the other hand, if the "picture" of the candidate is negative and the index is low, then the application is rejected. In those cases where the index seems to contradict the Dean's "picture" of the candidate, the Dean studies the application more carefully, trying to eliminate the contradiction. An application that creates a very positive picture of the candidate may very well be accepted despite a seemingly low index. And an application that creates a very negative picture of the candidate may very well be rejected despite a very good index.

At "Rising Star," the administrators say that the school has no policy of "strict indexing" but give the impression that they do rely on the index in making their recommendations to the Dean and that the Dean takes into consideration the index in evaluating the fairness of their recommendations.

The Index in Perspective

The preceding discussion should serve to debunk a popular myth: law schools just look at your LSAT score and your GPA; they don't even read that other stuff. This is certainly not true for the four schools we have described, and we know of no school for which the statement is true. (We know of one school for which the statement was true during its first year of operation. With very limited administrative resources, the admissions office ordered all applications according to index, projected that it would need X students to fill its first class, calculated that it would need to send out N acceptances to get X students, and then sent acceptance letters to the top N applications on the list. No one read any applications. By the following year, however, a more rational selection process was in place.)

On the other hand, some candidates have the mistaken impression that they have a chance at every school regardless of their LSAT score and GPA. We often hear statements to the effect "I know that my LSAT is only in the 25th percentile and my GPA is only 2.7, but I think the University of Chicago will accept me because I worked part-time while I was in school." This reasoning is incorrect. Although law schools do consider factors other than the LSAT score and the GPA (such as part-time work during college), your LSAT score and your GPA are still a very important part of your application. A law school is not simply going to disregard them. Even those law schools advertising that their admissions decisions are "based on a wide variety of factors intended to describe the whole person" will turn you down if your LSAT or GPA is too low.

An easy way to get a feel for the importance of the LSAT score and the GPA is to consult a copy of "The Official Guide to U.S. Law Schools" published by Law Services. Many law schools supply the "Official Guide" with LSAT score/GPA acceptance profile tables. These tables indicate how many applications a law school received with a certain LSAT score and a certain GPA and how many of those applications were accepted. A typical chart is shown on page 19.

If you study the chart, you will see that the data support two important conclusions:

1. Factors other than GPA and LSAT score are important to this school. Some applicants were turned down while other applicants who were seemingly less well-qualified (in terms of GPA and LSAT score) were accepted. For example, the school received applications from 515 candidates with GPAs in the range 3.25–3.49 and LSAT scores in the 81st–90th percentiles. It accepted only about half of those candidates—267 with those numerical qualifications were rejected. Yet the adjacent squares clearly show that some candidates with a lower GPA and/or LSAT score than those 267 were accepted.

The only feasible explanation for this phenomenon is that this law school looks at factors other than the GPA and the LSAT score. "Super numbers" are not a guarantee of admission, and somewhat lower numbers may not be an absolute bar. That's the good news. Now for the bad news.

2. The data also show that this school has some minimum standard for GPA and LSAT score. No candidate was admitted whose LSAT score fell below the 30 percentile, and no candidate was admitted whose GPA was lower than 2.5. And though some candidates were admitted whose LSAT scores were between the 31st percentile and the 70th percentile and whose GPAs were between 2.50 and 3.24, the overwhelming number of candidates with numbers in those ranges were rejected.

LSAT Percentile	0–10		11–20		21–30		31–40		41–50		51–60		61–70		71–80		81–90		91–99	
GPA	Apps	Adm	Apps	Adm	Apps	Adm	Apps	Adm	Apps	Adm	Apps	Adm	Apps	Adm	Apps	Adm	Apps	Adm	Apps	Adm
3.75+	3	0	3	0	6	0	8	1	10	1	43	4	39	12	61	42	88	81	89	86
3.50-3.74	2	0	12	0	21	0	24	2	26	1	121	8	127	21	158	76	272	213	213	201
3.25-3.49	9	0	26	0	50	0	48	3	75	2	215	15	215	13	307	84	515	267	369	289
3.00-3.24	19	0	39	0	62	0	68	1	110	5	219	12	127	3	264	21	421	52	315	82
2.75-2.99	25	0	50	0	48	0	51	2	83	1	152	6	80	4	139	7	248	11	186	16
2.50-2.74	24	0	43	0	39	0	39	1	69	1	56	4	26	1	68	5	107	4	77	6
2.25-2.49	36	0	28	0	27	0	20	0	8	0	8	0	12	0	29	0	52	0	24	0
2.00-2.24	12	0	13	0	8	0	6	0	9	0	4	0	8	0	7	0	18	0	11	0
Below 2.00	7	0	6	0	2	0	4	0	2	0	6	0	2	0	1	0	5	0	4	0

We can't tell from the data whether or not there is a formal minimum for GPA and LSAT score at this school, and most law schools deny that they have any "official" minimum GPA or LSAT score for admission. But if no candidate with numbers below a certain level is accepted then that school has *de facto* if not *de jure* minimums for GPA and LSAT score. Those candidates who were admitted with strikingly low numbers probably had unique qualifications or were admitted under some special program.

In summary, we can say that most law schools have at least informal minimums for GPA and LSAT score. Above those minimums, factors other than the GPA and the LSAT score can become important. What those factors are we will see in the next section.

THE LAW SCHOOL'S PERSPECTIVE

Before you continue your reading, take a moment to answer the following question:

What are the three most important qualities that admissions officers look for in a law school applicant?

1.

2.

3.

When we ask this question at our application workshops, the first person recognized almost invariably answers that "leadership ability" is the most important factor. This answer, while frequently offered, is wrong, as you will understand.

In this section, we want to get you to see the admissions process from the perspective of the law schools. Seeing the issues in this way will help you decide what to say in your application and how to say it. So, imagine that you are the director of admissions of a law school. Each year the school receives five times as many applications as there are seats available in the next year's entering class. How would you decide which applications to accept and which to turn down?

You must keep in mind that as an admissions officer you have responsibilities—to your applicants, to the school, and to society. Each of these responsibilities will influence the way you make your admissions decisions.

First, with regard to your applicants, would you want to admit a student who, you suspected, simply was not capable of graduating? Obviously not. To admit a candidate who would surely fail would do a disservice to that candidate, who would lose a great deal in terms of money, time, and probably self-esteem.

The same conclusion is dictated by the interest of the school. Would the faculty be very happy with a student who could not keep up? Again, the answer is surely no. From the standpoint of the school's budget, do you think that the dean, who has budgeted for faculty salaries and classroom space, would be very happy if a significant number of students flunked out and therefore stopped paying tuition? Again, no. Or would the entire school be better served by good students who later become good lawyers and make nice contributions to the school's foundation fund? Certainly!

Finally, as a director of admissions for a law school, you would also want to be acutely aware of the influence your decisions may have on the structure of society. Law is surely one of the most powerful forces working to structure our society; and, as we said in Chapter 1, virtually all new lawyers have graduated from an ABA-accredited law school. The chances of becoming a lawyer by any other route are slim. Thus, as an admissions director you are a gatekeeper, and your decisions about who passes through that gate are decisions about who will have access to the power wielded by lawyers. You would like to ensure that those who ultimately become lawyers are morally fit for the role and that they have a sense of professional and ethical responsibility. Also, you would want to ensure that every subgroup in the society has an equal opportunity to have its members represented in the profession of law.

Given these concerns, you would probably first read an application to determine whether or not the candidate has the ability to complete successfully the law school curriculum, which ability—you hope—would also help make the graduate a successful attorney. If the application is devoid of any evidence of ability, you would probably reject it—even if the candidate is the child of a large contributor to the school. (Seriously, we know of a couple of instances in which tempests were triggered in academic teapots because admissions committees voted to reject the child of a faculty member.)

What would constitute evidence of ability? First, the past academic record of the applicant and the GPA are convenient, readily available measures of past academic ability. But course requirements and standards of grading vary from school to school. The LSAT is designed to give admissions officers an "objective" standard that avoids these difficulties. To be sure, the LSAT is not a perfect testing instrument, and the sponsors of the exams are always at pains to make sure that law school admissions officers understand the limitations of the LSAT. But law school admissions officers are by and large satisfied that there is enough evidence of the LSAT's validity in predicting law school performance, and they use it.

We can see now that institutional considerations—the importance of finding students with the requisite academic ability—would lead an admissions officer to rely on the GPA and the LSAT. Thus, the pattern we saw in the preceding section is naturally explained by reference to these considerations. But other considerations show the limitations on these factors.

A Grade Point Average is, as the phrase indicates, an average, and an average does not convey certain information about a candidate's ability that you, as an admissions officer, might want to use in making your decision. It would be important to know, for example, whether there was any trend to an applicant's grades. A GPA might be pulled down by one or two unrepresentative semesters. Some students require a longer time than others to adjust to the rigors of college study. Their later grades are likely to be much higher than their freshman marks, but the first-year results will pull down the overall GPA. As an admissions officer, you might be willing to discount those earlier grades and rely more heavily on the later performance as being a better indicator of a candidate's ability. And you would certainly want to discount a single unrepresentative semester, particularly if the candidate can explain that circumstances such as personal illness or a death in the family interfered with studying that semester.

You would also want to look closely at a candidate's transcript to determine the quality of work that was needed to generate the candidate's GPA. As you examine the transcript, you would try to determine whether the mix of courses taken was academically challenging and whether there were any especially difficult individual courses. It would also be a good idea to learn something about the life experiences that surrounded the candidate's undergraduate study. Factors such as part-time work or family responsibilities would be important in interpreting what the GPA means in terms of ability.

Would you place any weight on graduate study? Yes: to the extent that a candidate's graduate marks either supported or contradicted the conclusion suggested by the undergraduate GPA, this information could be important. If a candidate with a relatively low undergraduate GPA had returned to school as a more mature person and done very well, you would probably conclude that the latter performance at the graduate level is better evidence of that person's ability than the earlier undergraduate marks.

Other aspects of an applicant's background might also suggest the presence of ability: extensive work experience with significant professional accomplishments, achievements in extracurricular activities, or community service.

The point so far is that you, as director of admissions, would want to be satisfied—for the sake of the applicant and for the sake of the school—that the applicant has the raw "intellectual horsepower" to get the job done. But that is not the end of your inquiry. Do you know anyone who is truly gifted but rarely puts those talents to use? We all do. Ability alone is not enough. There has to be a commitment to the educational process. It would be very risky indeed to accept a candidate with top numbers who says "I don't really want to go to law school, but I think I'll try it for a while to see if I like it."

What kind of evidence might there be of commitment or motivation? Past academic and professional success are strongly suggestive of commitment and motivation. Or, an applicant just might be able to spell out the reasons why he or she wants to go to law school. Would that reason have to be something like "I want to reform the world?" No. To be sure, if someone has a specific project in mind, such as Legal Aid, and has a background to suggest that this is a real intent, then that could be very persuasive evidence for the conclusion that the candidate is highly motivated. But equally persuasive might be a stated intention to work for a large corporate firm. Most admissions officers will be less concerned about the "political correctness" of a candidate's career plans than the sincerity and intensity with which the commitment is felt.

Thus far, we have decided that you would want to see strong evidence of both ability and commitment. Ability without commitment is just raw energy without direction and is doomed to failure. Without ability, commitment, no matter how sincerely and strongly felt, is impotent. Both qualities are necessary.

Now let us suppose that you receive 5,000 applications for the 250 seats in next year's entering class. And let us assume that you can safely eliminate 1,000 candidates because they don't seem to have the needed ability or motivation or perhaps both. Of the remaining candidates, a few stand out as superstars, and you will of course want to accept them. You still have about four times as many applications as you can accept, and you have satisfied yourself that each of them can successfully do the work. You could fill the remaining seats just by taking those with the best LSAT scores and GPAs. That, however, lacks imagination.

If you had a choice between two candidates, both with very similar numbers and academic background, one a retired professional baseball player and the other a college senior with nothing interesting in the resumé, which candidate would you prefer? Yes, admissions officers are also looking to put together an interesting group of people who will bring with them different perspectives.

Now, as director of admissions, you have yet another responsibility—that to society. For some people, you may use different criteria. You will still look for ability and commitment, but the evidence of those factors may be different in some applications. A 3.5 GPA is not just a 3.5. It is a 3.5 that was earned by a person in very specific circumstances. And a 3.5 earned under adverse circumstances shows more ability than a 3.5 earned under circumstances very conducive to learning. Additionally, you may have reason to believe that the LSAT doesn't have the same validity for all groups in the applicant pool. If, for example, you have determined that the LSAT underpredicts the performance of certain minority candidates, you would adjust your thinking for those candidates. You wouldn't change your goal of finding qualified and motivated students, but you would interpret the evidence provided by the LSAT differently. Since the LSAT is in a sense defective when applied to these candidates, you might apply a different standard in certain cases.

As you can begin to appreciate, the admissions decision is complex, and you would want as much relevant information as possible. To that end, you might want to give applicants a chance to submit personal statements and would invite them to do so. Additionally, it would be highly desirable though not really practical to talk with those people who know the candidate best. As a substitute, you might ask that the candidate arrange for two or three people to write to you and give you their opinions about the applicant.

Would this additional input always be helpful? No. Some candidates misunderstand your job as an admissions officer and would write personal statements and arrange for letters that would not be helpful for any number of reasons. Those candidates, however, who understand what is required for you to accept an application can supply information that helps you evaluate their applications. And, in doing so, they will improve their own chances of admissions.

In chapters four and five, we talk about completing the application, writing the personal statement, and arranging for letters of evaluation. The strategies we will suggest are all developed from an understanding of the admissions process from the perspective of the law school itself.

CHAPTER 3

TARGETING SCHOOLS

In Chapter 1, we explained why most people considering the law as a career should focus exclusively on law schools that have received accreditation (either full or provisional) from the American Bar Association. However, it is obviously necessary to narrow the focus of inquiry and to target a group of schools smaller than the 175 institutions on the ABA's approved list.

To some extent, the choice of target schools may be limited by personal, professional, or financial concerns. Family ties may dictate geographical limitations. Professional responsibilities may require the student to seek out law schools within commuting distance that offer part-time programs that suit very specific scheduling needs. A concern about debt management may suggest application to only state-supported schools in order to take advantage of the lower tuition they offer.

Even within these limitations, there is a wide array of law schools from which to choose. (See Appendix C.) The general remarks of this chapter may be easily adapted to a specific situation.

Special circumstances aside, the question "Where should I apply?" is an important one to all law school applicants. From our own experience teaching admissions seminars and workshops, we have learned that most people are willing to cast their application nets fairly wide. Their attitude commonly is "I want to get into the best school I can and will go wherever that 'best' school happens to be located." While this chapter contains information that is of interest to virtually every prospective law student (e.g., a listing of "top" schools), it will be most useful to those with no personal constraints.

AIMING HIGH

One strategy for targeting schools is "apply to the best and hope for the best," that is, apply to the best schools at which you have a reasonable chance of admission. But that strategy requires a ranking system that establishes which schools are better than others.

The Ranking Controversy

Some authorities in legal education view the question about "best schools" as a specious one because it is in principle unanswerable. They point out that the word "best" does not have a single, univocal meaning. After all, what is best for one student may not be best for another. One student may be best suited by a high-powered big-name school with large classes and a proven record of placing its graduates in large firms in major cities. For another student, "best" may mean a smaller school with more personal contact with faculty and the opportunity to work part time for a solo practitioner in a small town. So, since there is no agreement on the criteria by which to measure law schools, no ranking of schools is possible.

This is the line of reasoning used by the American Bar Association to condemn categorically any attempt to rank law schools:

> *No rating of law schools beyond the simple statement of their accreditation is attempted or advocated by the official organizations in legal education. Qualities that make one kind of school good for one student may not be as important to another. The American Bar Association and its Section of Legal Education and Admissions to the Bar have issued disclaimers of any law school rating system.* *

On the academic side, the Law School Admission Council (the non-profit association of American and Canadian Law Schools), through its operating arm, Law School Admissions Services, Inc., implicitly defers to the ABA as the proper authority for any official ranking and does not offer a ranking system of its own. LSAS does acknowledge that factors such as reputation, placement record, and faculty tend to create a public perception of a hierarchy, then notes that such factors are difficult to quantify. LSAS concludes that since there is no "official ranking authority," caution should be exercised in consulting any system of rankings.**

On the other hand, rankings are available, and they are very popular.

---

*The American Bar Association, Statement 20, *Policies of the Council of the Section of Legal Education and Admission to the Bar and of the Accreditation Committee* (Indianapolis, IN: 1987), p. 18.
**Law School Admissions Services, Inc., *The Official Guide to U.S. Law Schools, 1992–1993,* p. 19.

U.S. News and World Report, which publishes an annual survey that ranks all of the law schools in the country, indicates that its "rankings issue" is one of the best selling of the year. The magazine's ranking system incorporates variables such as "LSAT score of entering students" and "average starting salary of recent graduates." The magazine even commissions surveys of law school deans and judges to measure "academic reputation" and "professional reputation." The resulting list with its many footnotes and explanation of methodology is a fairly impressive presentation of a ranking, a ranking that the ABA says is impossible.

Which position on the rankings issue is correct? Certainly the ABA is correct to point out that "best" may mean different things to different students—that point is hardly controversial. And *U.S. News* is at pains to explain in some detail what factors were used to identify the "best" law schools and how they were weighted. As for Law Service's position, it is difficult to quarrel with the advice to exercise caution when consulting a ranking, but that advice is good regardless of whether there exists an "official" ranking. After all, would you blindly accept a listing of "best automobiles" simply because the list had been compiled by some organization of car manufacturers?

Using a Ranking

We agree with some of what the ABA says: "Best" doesn't mean the same thing to every law school candidate. And we agree with part of what Law Services has to say: Read any survey with a skeptical eye. But we think that a ranking can be a useful tool for choosing which law schools to apply to. When consulting any ranking, you should keep a number of points in mind.

One, you should read carefully the explanation of the way that the ranking was calculated. A ranking of any sophistication will incorporate several factors—some of which may be important to you, others not. You should also pay careful attention to the method for weighting the factors. Indeed, you might want to use the data that support the ranking to make your own ranking by creating a different mix of factors or by assigning the factors different weights.

Two, and this point is extremely important, the seeming precision of the linear order of the ranking is an *illusion*! In the first place, a slight adjustment in the mix of the factors used to calculate the ranking or their relative weights would almost surely change many positions in the order, moving schools down or up the scale by several positions; and the adjusted ranking would look very different from the original one. Further, not all schools report the same statistical gauges. Some law schools, for example, keep a record of the *median* starting salary of graduates, while others keep a record of the *average* starting salary; and the two different measures are not completely interchangeable. Also, several law schools do not make public average LSAT scores or GPAs of applicants or entering students. Thus, some of the data used to create a ranking may have been derived by estimation rather than from a survey response. Finally, the data given to rankings surveys are subject to the vagaries of the information-gathering process, e.g., how many of that year's graduates responding to the law school's survey on placement were candid.

The best way to use a ranking is to regard each school's position in the list as a range rather than a precise rank. Thus, the "true" rank of the top school is somewhere in the top four or five, while that of the number-ten school is somewhere between six and 15.

Three, the fact that a law school is not included in a list of the "Top 25" doesn't necessarily mean that it doesn't belong on the list. Rather, schools are left off simply because that list has only 25 positions. There may very well be a couple of dozen other schools with rankings so close to those of number 25 that a slight change in the weighting or method of calculating different factors could displace several lower-ranking members from the list. Don't automatically assume that a school that does not appear on the short list is not the equal of some of the schools that do appear.

The Best Law Schools

Recently, we finished a directory entitled *The Best Law Schools.* Its plan was to treat in detail a limited number of law schools, so it was necessary to have some method by which to identify the schools to be included. Our strategy was to defer to some authoritative ranking of law schools prepared by a professional organization or an academic body.

Since no official ranking was available, we decided to create our own system from scratch. We were not deterred by the ABA's objection that "best" might mean different things for different people. After all, most people who consult comparative rankings of any product or service do not expect that the analysis will be tailored to their unique circumstances. People who ask about the "best" law schools are not expecting the names of law schools judged best by some absolute standard nor the names of those best suited to their individual circumstances. Rather, what they ask is a ranking system be *serviceable*—that it be factually reliable and that it employ reasonable standards.

---

*Thomas H. Martinson, *The Best Law Schools* (Prentice Hall: New York, 1993).

Our method of gathering data was to ask the law schools themselves through a survey questionnaire. Of course, even this method of data gathering has shortcomings, but given that the information is under the control of the law schools, a survey questionnaire seemed best calculated to produce reliable information. The next task was to create a *reasonable* ranking system; and over the years, we have learned that when people ask "What are the best law schools?", they generally expect an answer that ranks schools according to three criteria: admissions selectivity, educational effectiveness, and placement power.

To measure selectivity, we used median LSAT score and GPA of entering students. After all, if those measures can be used by admissions officers to identify the "best" law school applicants, it seems equally fair to use them to identify the "best" law schools. Another measure is the ratio of acceptances to applications. The lower the ratio, the more difficult it is to gain admission to that school.

Measuring educational effectiveness was more problematic. Even when a certain law school's graduates continually demonstrate professional excellence, should one conclude that it was the law school's training that made the difference? Indeed, it is sometimes claimed that the so-called top law schools really don't provide a better legal education than any other schools; they just get the best students. After graduation, those students, who would likely have become successful no matter where they were educated, do indeed go on to become successful, and the law school unjustly claims responsibility for their success.

Setting that suggestion aside, but recognizing the difficulty in finding measures of educational effectiveness, we finally decided to use judicial clerkships, one- or two-year assistantships to a judge. Competition for judicial clerkships, particularly with prestigious courts, can be extremely stiff. A judge's offer of clerkship is an implicit recognition by a leading legal authority that the candidate has received a top-notch legal education. Our ranking system used the percent of each school's graduating class who accept clerkships with the U.S. Supreme Court, a U.S. Court of Appeals, a U.S. District Court, or a state's highest court as the measure of a law school's educational effectiveness.

Finally, a law school's placement power can be measured fairly directly by the percentage of students in a graduating class who have jobs at graduation. And, of course, median starting salary is also a measure of a law school's placement success.

So, our ranking of "best" law schools used these criteria:

- As measures of selectivity: median LSAT score; median college GPA; and acceptance/application ratio.
- As a measure of educational effectiveness: percent of graduates placed in certain judicial clerkships.

- As measures of placement power: percentage placed at graduation and median starting salary.

We prescreened law schools using published admissions data and
mailed out 51 questionnaires. We received a return of 40 completed
questionnaires. Using this data, we awarded the schools points
based on their standing according to each of the six specific measures. The top-ranked school on the list received the maximum number of points (a number equal to the number of schools in the list),
the second-ranked school received one point less than the top-
ranked school, and so on. (In cases of ties, points were distributed
equally among the schools tied.) For Selectivity and Placement,
scores were simply averages of the scores for each of the specific
measures for that criterion. Educational effectiveness was just the
clerkship ranking. The overall ranking was the average of scores of
each of the three criteria.

After identifying the top 25 schools according to these criteria, we
recalculated rankings for those 25 in the same way to generate a
refined listing. Here is that listing:

1. Yale University
2. University of Chicago
3. Harvard University
4. Stanford University
5. New York University
6. Columbia University
7. University of Michigan
8. University of California—
   Berkeley
9. University of Virginia
10. Northwestern University
11. University of Pennsylvania
12. Duke University
13. Vanderbilt University
14. Cornell University
15. University of Southern
    California
16. Georgetown University
17. University of California—
    Davis
18. Fordham University
19. College of William & Mary
20. Washington & Lee
    University
21. University of Washington
22. University of North
    Carolina
23. University of Minnesota
24. University of Texas
25. University of Notre Dame

The other 15 schools ranked in the top 40 were (in alphabetical order):

Boston College
Boston University

University of California—
Hastings

Case Western Reserve University	University of Illinois, Urbana-Champaign
University of Colorado—Boulder	Indiana University—Bloomington
Emory University	The Ohio State University
University of Florida	University of Utah
George Washington University	University of Wisconsin—Madison
Hofstra University	Yeshiva University

OTHER FACTORS

The ranking system that we used is fairly simple, but to most people it will probably seem reasonable and accessible. However, there are some factors that we might have used that were left out. You may want to consider these other factors when making your own comparisons of law schools. And you may also want to know why we did not use them in our ranking system.

Reputation

If you talk to people in the legal field about what they think of various law schools, you will immediately encounter several difficulties. First, most practitioners will be familiar with only a very few schools, and the opinions you get may just be impressions of someone else's impressions. Second, reputations change; and if you talk to someone who graduated from law school 10 or 20 years ago, you may get an opinion that is no longer justified.

Third, and perhaps most important, what is the value of "reputation"? Suppose that there exists a law school with an excellent reputation. It has big-name professors, a huge library, and students with very high LSAT scores and GPAs—but its graduates, though all brilliant, just can't get jobs. Would you want to enroll at that school? Obviously not.

Of course, such a school does not exist. But what the above demonstrates is that "reputation" is an imprecise term for what people really mean by other, concrete factors such as "placement power." A law school's reputation is an imperfect reflection of its selectivity, educational effectiveness, and placement power. So instead of searching for an ephemeral and unquantifiable notion such as "reputation," we chose to emphasize the more concrete factors outlined above.

Student/Faculty Ratio

The suggestion that a law school's student/faculty ratio is a measure of the educational effectiveness of the school has a certain prima facie plausibility: more teachers equal better education. This equation may or may not be true for several reasons.

First, law schools employ many different types of teachers and list their faculty in different ways. Some schools include "adjunct professors," usually part-time teachers who have full-time professional responsibilities elsewhere, often as practicing lawyers. This is not to say that adjunct professors are not good teachers. In fact, they may be some of the best teachers at the law school, because they are actually engaged in the practice of law on a day-to-day basis. On the other hand, because they have full-time obligations outside the law school, they may not be readily available to students outside of class. Faculty listings may also include "Deans," "Law Librarians," and even professors "Emeriti." If you compare law schools according to teacher-to-student ratios, be sure the ratios are comparable by counting only those faculty members who have a title such as Assistant Professor, Associate Professor, or Professor of Law.

Second, the learning experience in law school is radically different from that of college or even graduate school. First-year classes routinely include 100 or more students. The give-and-take among many students in large classes often enhances the first-year experience. Law schools also balance these large first-year classes with small groups, and upper-division offerings include seminar classes. Also, much of what you learn in law school you will learn on your own in the library or from your classmates through informal discussions. Thus, faculty accessibility does not have the same value in law school that it has in other settings.

Finally, law schools are justifiably proud of their "big guns," professors who have written important works, have held high-profile positions prior to joining the faculty, or still hold important positions. Again, however, we despaired of quantifying the additional value of such individuals and of finding a measure for the best mix of teachers. Indeed, it was not even clear to us that "big guns" are a positive addition to a faculty from the standpoint of student learning.

Books, Bricks, and Computers

Another way of comparing law schools is by their library holdings, and it is certainly true that the better schools will have better libraries. Measuring library quality, however, is difficult. "Total volumes," for example, is at best a very crude measure of a library's effectiveness, for the measure does not focus on those books that are most important to students—books such as case reporters and reference works.

Another aspect of library effectiveness is what might be called "seating capacity" or even "user friendliness." The value to an individual student of an assigned study carrel with a locked cabinet for storing personal belongings can be very great, but finding a measure of that value seemed to us to be impossible.

Finally, legal research increasingly includes a computer-assisted component. Thus, the number of terminals and printers and the number of hours students are permitted to use computerized search is yet another determinant of a library's effectiveness. A law school that has extensive computerized research facilities obviously has a lot of money to spend on its library, strong evidence that the library is a good one.

Law School Catalogues

Although law school catalogues are an important source of information, it is important to keep in mind who prepared them. A school's catalogue was written to attract "business," and you can bet that it was carefully phrased to present the law school in its best light.

Consider the following claims regarding class composition, library resources, and placement made by a school we will designate L.S. A:

- Total enrollment is about 1,000 students, including students from 42 states and several foreign countries.
- In the library, LEXIS and WESTLAW terminals are available for computerized legal research.
- Over 90 percent of recent graduates currently work in law or law-related fields.
- With approximately 10 applicants for each seat in the entering class, admission is very competitive.

These claims describe some very good points of this law school: the school has a diverse student body; it has computerized research facilities; and its graduates are able to find jobs. Now, contrast the claims above with the following claims made by a school we will designate L.S. B:

- Last year's entering class of 300 included students from over 42 different states and from several foreign countries.
- LEXIS and WESTLAW terminals are available at numerous locations throughout the law school for independent use.
- At the time of graduation, 90 percent of the students who wanted a job in law or a law-related field had one.
- Last year's entering class of 300 was chosen from a pool of 3,000 applications.

These claims, though similar to those of the first law school, are much stronger.

As for the claim regarding class diversity, L.S. A bases its claim on its entire enrollment. L.S. B has just as much diversity in a single class as the first has in its entire student body. As for the second claim, L.S. A points out that it has modern computer resources in the library, but L.S. B notes that it makes computer resources available in various locations. And as for the claim regarding placement, L.S. A aggregates its "recent" graduates. One reason for phrasing the claim in this way may be to avoid publicizing the fact that it takes the school's graduates several months to find positions. L.S. B states specifically what happened to the most recent graduating class upon graduation.

The claim regarding selectivity is particularly interesting. At first glance, both schools may appear to be making the same claim, for the ratio cited is 10:1 in both cases. In fact, L.S. B is much more selective than L.S. A, though you cannot possibly learn this fact from the claims themselves. At L.S. A, one out of every three applications was accepted, at L.S. B only one out of every seven. Why the difference? Most people apply to several schools. So not every applicant who is accepted by a law school will elect to matriculate at that school. In order to ensure a sufficient number of acceptances to fill the entering class, a school must accept more applicants than it has available seats. Once accepted, an applicant accepted by L.S. B is much more likely to enroll at L.S. B than an applicant accepted by L.S. A is to enroll at L.S. A. We conclude, therefore, that L.S. B is much more selective.

DECIDING WHERE TO APPLY

We are often asked by applicants, "Which schools should I apply to?" We respond with another question: "How many do you plan to apply to?" And if asked, "How many should I apply to?," we would respond, "Which would you like to apply to?" There is a circularity here, because it is impossible to answer one of the questions independently of the other.

In one respect, an answer to the "how many" question depends on an answer to the "where" question. For a very strong candidate who plans to focus on a few top schools, the answer is "just a few." For a candidate with above-average but not outstanding qualifications who wants to get into a top school, the answer is "many." For a candidate with average qualifications who wants to attend a particular local school for which the qualifications are more than acceptable, the answer is just that one school (plus an insurance school or two). For a candidate with marginal qualifications who really wants to go to law school, the answer is "as many as you can afford."

On the other hand, an answer to the "where" question may also depend upon an answer to the "how many" question. A candidate with only limited resources who plans to submit only two or three applications must be very conservative and apply to schools at which the chances for acceptance are very, very good. But a candidate with unlimited resources can afford to apply to dozens of schools, including some for which the chances for acceptance are fairly slim.

For most people, finalizing a list of schools requires a trade-off. On the one hand, candidates want to get into the "best" school they can. On the other hand, most people cannot afford to apply to every ABA-accredited school. So you have to balance both competing considerations: In light of what you are able to spend, what mix of schools maximizes your chances of getting into the best possible school while still ensuring that you will be accepted by some schools?

On the average, candidates submit about four or five applications. That few applications won't give you very much flexibility in creating your list of target schools. Our recommendation is that you start targeting schools on the assumption that you will be applying to ten schools. Study the "Official Guide" and come up with a tentative list of ten schools. At that point, if you feel that there are other schools you want to include (and can afford the application fees), then expand the list. If you can't afford to apply to ten (or simply don't want to), then decide which schools you want most and pare down the list accordingly.

Ultimately, your list of target schools should be a mix of schools:

- A couple of "long shot" or "reach" schools
- A couple of "sure thing" schools
- Several "bread and butter" schools

"Long shot" or "reach" schools are schools for which your chances are not very good—perhaps only one out of five or even one out of ten—but which have good "reputations." A "sure thing" school is a school for which you almost seem overqualified: Your chances for acceptance are 80 percent or better. And "bread and butter" schools are those at which your numbers match, more or less, the average numbers of the most recent entering class.

The three categories of schools must be interpreted according to your numbers. At the very top, for a candidate with a 4.0 GPA and a perfect LSAT score, there are no "reach schools." Even the top schools are this candidate's "bread and butter" schools. Nonetheless, for this candidate, we still recommend applying to some "safe" schools. For a candidate with relatively less competitive numbers, say a 2.6 GPA and an LSAT score in the 40th percentile, there may very well be no "safe" schools. Schools that many people would consider their "bread and butter" schools are this candidate's "reach" schools, and this candidate may have to work to get admitted at even one or two schools.

As we stressed in Chapter 2, LSAT score and GPA are not the only factors considered by law school admissions officers. The "unquantifiables" are also very important. But keep in mind that the quantitative factors may be used to screen applications. If an application has quantitative measures that are too low, the applicant's "unquantifiables" may never even come to light.

As you work on your list of target schools, it will be necessary for you to try to anticipate how your "unquantifiables" will be weighed (see Chapter 2). Unfortunately, it is impossible to predict exactly how the description of your personal experiences will affect a given admissions officer. Our best advice on this score is: Be realistic.

When we do live admissions workshops and seminars, we ask for a show of hands from those in attendance to indicate how many have significant work experience and extracurricular activities. Here is what usually happens:

We say: "Everyone who has ever had a full-time or a part-time job, please raise your hand. (Every hand is up.)
"Now, everyone who has ever had two such jobs keep your hands up; everyone else put your hand down. (Almost every hand is up.)
"Next, everyone who considers that this work experience is "not very significant" lower your hand. (Virtually no hands go down.)
"Everyone please put your hands down, and then everyone with at least one significant extracurricular or community activity raise your hand again. (Virtually everyone raises a hand.)
"Everyone with two or more significant extracurricular activities keep your hands up, the rest of you can lower yours. (Very few hands are lowered.)
"And the same for people with three or more significant activities. (Most people still have a hand raised.)

This little experiment, repeated many times over the past years, suggests that most people applying to law school have significant extracurricular/community activities and work experience (and perhaps that some applicants wrongly consider their work experience and extracurricular/community service activities to be significant). The results of the experiment are not surprising. After all, the pool is literally filled with very competitive applicants.

MISCELLANEOUS CONSIDERATIONS

The Bar Exam

Upon completion of your law school studies, you will be awarded the degree of Juris Doctor; but holding that degree does not automatically make you an attorney. To become an attorney, you must first apply to the board of bar examiners in the state or states in which you wish to practice law for admission to the bar. After the application is approved, you can then be sworn in as an attorney.

Each jurisdiction has its own procedures for admitting new attorneys; but, in general, in addition to holding a law degree you must also pass that state's bar exam and prove to the committee of bar examiners that you are morally fit to practice law. It is the bar exam requirement that you may want to consider when choosing law schools.

Most law schools, particularly those that have national reputations and draw students from many different states, don't teach the law of any particular jurisdiction. Rather, they are concerned with teaching analytical skills and general legal concepts. A student who graduates from a top school on the East Coast is not necessarily equipped to take the bar exam in California, and vice versa. In fact, we have reliable information about a Yale graduate (and law review editor) at a top New York firm who failed the New York bar exam five times!

On the other hand, some schools, particularly those that draw most of their students from a single state or an otherwise limited area, do offer courses in the law of that particular state. These schools are often able to boast that their students have a far better pass rate on their states' bar exams than the students of the "big name" schools. Until you have passed the bar exam and have been admitted to the practice of law, your value to an employer will be limited. Many employers, including private firms and government agencies, condition hiring, continued employment, and salary raises on a person's admission to the practice of law.

Don't give the bar exam requirement more weight than it deserves. Most states have pass rates of 70 percent to 75 percent or even higher. A bar review course will be available to teach you what you need to know about the law of a particular state. And, most states will allow you to take the bar exam until you finally pass. (A few states have a limit on the number of times a candidate can take the bar exam without special permission.)

Part-Time Programs

Some sixty-plus law schools offer part-time programs. If you anticipate that you will need to work full-time while in law school, then you will need to look for a part-time law school program: ABA rules on accreditation limit the number of hours a full-time student may work during the academic year. Whereas full-time programs require three years of study, part-time programs require at least four years. In recent history, part-time students have accounted for a little less than one-fifth of all law school enrollments.

We suggest that anyone considering a part-time program think very seriously about what will be required in terms of the time commitment, intellectual energy that will be expended, and the threat to personal well-being. Imagine putting in a full day at the office, traveling to school, sitting through three hours of classes, and arriving home at ten or eleven o'clock—in time to go to bed in order to get just enough sleep to start over again the next morning. You can spend your weekends catching up on your casebook reading.

We do not mean to imply that this regimen is impossible. Indeed, we admire the tens of thousands of students who have the mental and physical strength to accomplish this grueling task. But don't shy away from the possibility of full-time study just because you may have to borrow money. Most people find a way to finance a full-time study program using grants, loans, and part-time and summer employment. And remember that with a full-time program you will qualify for a lawyer's salary a year earlier than if you take a part-time program.

One final point should be made about part-time versus full-time study. People often wonder whether it is easier to get into a part-time than a full-time program. In general, part-time programs are *slightly* less competitive than full-time programs. But this does not mean that you should apply to a particular school's part-time program rather than its full-time program in hopes of maximizing your chances of getting into that school. In the first place, the difference in selectivity is only slight. In the second place, since so many factors are taken into account in the admissions decision, you have no way of knowing whether that slight difference would make a difference in your case. So don't forgo the advantages of full-time study for an advantage in admissions that may not be an advantage at all.

Curriculum

You will probably find it very difficult to distinguish law schools on the basis of curriculum, for most catalogues contain substantially the same offerings. The typical first-year curriculum includes the core courses that teach basic legal concepts in the traditional areas of criminal law, civil procedure, property law, torts, and contracts, with a moot court requirement and an elective or two.

Second- and third-year students are usually offered a choice from among old standards such as Constitutional law, corporations, labor law, administrative law, antitrust law, taxation, evidence, estate planning, domestic relations, etc. And the offerings may include the specialties of some faculty members (such as a seminar on English legal history or election law) and courses in more recent developments in the law (such as environmental law or computer law).

There are three types of programs, however, that could make a difference to you. First, many schools offer joint degree programs that combine study in areas such as business or public administration with the study of law. Taking a joint degree can be cheaper and less time-consuming than taking two consecutive degrees.

Second, some schools offer more extensive clinical programs than others, and practical experience can be a big plus when you start practicing law. Years ago, most law schools didn't offer such programs. The closest a student usually got to the actual practice of law was moot court and some summer employment. This state of affairs led to the cynical question: "Where is the court house?" The question was a slap at students who were well-schooled in theory but had no practical training whatsoever.

Clearly, a clinical program can be a valuable part of a legal education, but again we remind you to read law school catalogues carefully. The term "clinical program" might arguably be applied to any practical legal training, perhaps even including the traditional moot court. Make sure that the law school's definition of a clinical program coincides with your expectations: Who are the clients? How much responsibility are students given? How much supervision by faculty or attorneys do students get? How much academic credit is given for participation?

Third, many schools offer concentrations in areas such as sports law, entertainment law, and environmental law. Such concentrations may be valuable, and many schools can justifiably boast of having assembled a group of faculty who have broken new ground or who have special credentials in such areas. Two caveats, however, are in order. One, as always, read the law school catalogue carefully. Make sure you will be getting what you expect, e.g., how many courses are offered in the specialization? Two, you shouldn't overestimate the value of such concentrations. The issues that arise in specialty areas also arise routinely in most other areas of the law—issues such as contractual relations, property rights, governmental procedure, and so on. Finally, an area of specialization may sound glamorous, but once you get into the legal concepts you may discover that the field is not really for you. In short, if you have prior experience in a special field and know that legal training with special emphasis in that area will help you, then that is a good reason for selecting a particular law school. But if you are entering law school with no definite post-graduation plans, do not give too much weight to the specializations offered by various law schools.

Environment

Our final factor is so obvious that some readers will wonder why we even mention it. Other readers will regard it as so important that they will wonder why we haven't devoted more space to it. Obviously, the geographical location of the school, its distance from or proximity to loved ones, the living conditions it offers, and the state of its physical plant are items to be considered. But since the interpretation of and weight given to these factors is so subjective, there is little assistance we can offer. We can only suggest that you keep the following points in mind.

First, law school takes three or (in the case of a part-time program) four years. Depending on your sensitivity to environmental factors, that can be either a very short or a very long time.

Second, if you are a full-time student, the focus of your social life is likely to be the law school itself, especially if you are single and live on campus. If you are married with children, then you will obviously have other social obligations. Even so, you may very well find that most of your social contacts are other law students with family.

Third, law school absorbs a great deal of time. So, many of the hours you may have spent as an undergraduate in the college's rathskeller or coffee house will likely be spent in the library's cellar or at home studying.

Fourth, law school is not prison. You do get summers and holidays off. And you might even be able to squeeze in an occasional weekend away from school.

In general, then, while environment is an important factor, don't overestimate its importance. Apply to schools that seem to be good choices, and then visit those that accept you to make sure that the surroundings are suitable.

CHAPTER **4**

COMPLETING THE APPLICATION

In this chapter, we discuss procedures for completing the law school application. By the term application, we do not mean just the application form. Rather, we mean all of the components that must be delivered to a law school before an application is considered complete. For most schools, a completed application must include the following:

LSAT score

LSDAS report

Dean's evaluation

Reference letters

Personal statement

Application form or forms

Application fee

(The personal statement is covered in the next chapter.)

You are responsible for initiating the application process. To arrange to take the LSAT and to register for LSDAS contact:

Law Services
Box 2000
661 Penn Street
Newtown, PA 18940-0998
Telephone: (215) 968-1001

To obtain application forms for particular schools, you must write or telephone those schools directly. A Law Services registration is *not* an application to a specific law school. Even though you direct Law Services to send your LSAT score and transcript information to particular law schools, you must contact those schools directly to receive application forms.

A law school application consists of several components. Each component requires several successive steps such as requesting information, completing forms, processing, etc. Some steps can take several weeks to complete. Failure to take a key step at the appropriate time can slow down the entire project and may fatally delay completion of the application. Successful orchestration of the various sections of the application requires advance planning and careful attention to detail.

THE APPLICATION CYCLE

The prototypical law school program involves three consecutive academic years of study. Under this type of program, students are admitted only in the fall and graduate about thirty-three months later. Some law schools do offer variations on this theme with programs such as mid-year admissions and summer terms. We will regard these as exceptions to the general rule and refer readers interested in such programs to the "Official Guide to U.S. Law Schools." Those readers will be able to adapt the general principles described below to fit any special case.

The typical law school begins to accept applications for its next entering class in October—almost a full year before the students in that class will start their studies. Deadlines for filing applications may come as early as February 1 of the year in which the applicant expects to enroll or as late as June 15 of that year. We will refer to this period as the "application season." (A few law schools don't have absolute deadlines and may be willing to consider applications right up until the time classes start or the time at which all seats are allocated, whichever comes first.)

Just as the length of its application season is set by each school, the timing of decisions and notifications varies from school to school. In the past, schools accumulated applications until the deadline for accepting applications had passed. Then all applications were reviewed together. Only at that time were decisions made and notifications sent. Today, many law schools use a "rolling" admissions process for decision-making. A law school that operates on the rolling admissions principle reviews applications from time to time all during application season. Based on a school's experience with applications in previous years, its admissions officers make projections of what its next entering class will look like in terms of LSAT scores, GPAs, etc. Then, as soon as a significant number of applications have been received, and in light of the projections, the review process begins. Some applicants are immediately accepted; some applicants are immediately rejected; other applicants are put into a "hold" category, and action is delayed until a more precise picture of the next entering class can be developed.

If you are thinking of applying to a school that uses rolling admissions, apply early in the season. As the admissions process "rolls" on through the season, acceptances are sent out and the number of available seats shrinks. Your chances are better if you apply early. (If you are already in the middle of the application season and have not yet filed applications even at schools that do use rolling admissions, don't panic! We are not suggesting that it is already too late. Your chances at certain schools may have been compromised somewhat, but this delay is not necessarily a disaster. You should go ahead and apply, but you may want to downgrade your chances slightly at schools that do use rolling admissions.)

At most law schools, all applications are ultimately either accepted or rejected. (A "wait list" disposition eventually matures into one of the other two.) About a dozen and a half schools, however, have a third possible disposition: provisional admission. A provisional admission invites an applicant who would otherwise be rejected to enroll at the school for a special summer program. Then, provided that the applicant's performance in the special summer course is satisfactory, the applicant is offered a seat in the entering fall class.

Law schools with provisional admission policies may be particularly attractive to those applicants who show academic promise according to some predictors but not others. When discussing their provisional admission programs, schools typically mention applicants with high GPAs but low LSAT scores and vice versa.

SCHEDULING THE LAW SCHOOL ADMISSION TEST

The LSAT is administered four times each year. The exact dates vary from year to year, but administrations are usually scheduled in the early fall, in the late fall, in mid-winter, and in late spring. Regular registration for the LSAT closes approximately five weeks before each test date. Late registration closes about two weeks before each test date. (Late registration requires payment of an additional fee.) Score reports become available about six weeks after each test administration.

We recommend that you take the LSAT *before* the start of the application season in which you plan to participate. Since the test is administered in the winter (usually February), the late spring (usually June), and the early autumn (usually October), our advice is to take the exam in the winter or spring—at least fifteen months prior to the time you plan to start law school.

With an LSAT score already "in the bank," you can use the summer to make some preliminary decisions about what schools you might be interested in and begin preparing the documentation for your applications. You will be in a position to complete and submit applications as soon as they become available in the fall.

Additionally, by taking the LSAT early, you build in a time cushion. If you plan to take the LSAT in the late spring but circumstances prevent you from doing so, you can take the early fall administration. Even though your score will not be available until November, your applications can still be submitted relatively early in the season. If you first schedule an LSAT administration in the early fall and are prevented from taking the test, the next opportunity won't be until the late fall. Your score won't be available until mid-January. As a consequence, you might miss some important application deadlines.

Of course, you should not carry this advice to extremes. There is no reason to take the LSAT several years in advance of making applications. In fact, there are two reasons not to do so. One, LSAT scores have a limited "shelf life." Although LSAS will carry an LSAT score on a candidate's score report for several years, most law schools regard a score that is more than two or three years old as "stale." If your score is too old, you will have to take the test again. Two, if you are currently an undergraduate, your reading ability and analytical skills may be maturing very rapidly. Waiting three to six months (until the late spring of your junior year) may very well enhance your performance on the test.

RETAKING THE LSAT

You may take the LSAT more than once. In fact, you may take it several times. But our advice is DO IT ONCE; DO IT RIGHT; AND DON'T DO IT AGAIN. The basis for this advice is the reporting system. Your score report will show each time you have taken the test and the result (a score or a score cancellation). Many schools average multiple scores. Others take a second higher score but discount it somewhat because candidates routinely improve slightly on a second testing because of a "familiarity" factor. Ideally, then, you want only your one, highest score.

If someone has already taken the LSAT and received a disappointing score or perhaps scores, is it advisable for that person to take the test again? Unfortunately, there is no single, clear-cut answer to this question because there is always the risk that another testing will result in the same or even a lower score. There are, however, circumstances that strongly suggest that another testing could be advantageous:

- External factors such as illness or emotional trauma interfered with performance on the earlier test.
- Random events such as miscoding the answer sheet or drastic misallocation of time invalidated performance on the earlier test.
- Lack of adequate preparation prevented maximum performance on the earlier test.

Indeed, law schools may be willing to discount an earlier, lower score if it can be explained in terms of external or random factors. (We don't suggest trying to explain a low score to a law school by claiming "lack of adequate preparation.")

Additionally, some law schools will take the most recent or the highest score. And many law schools will disregard an earlier score if a subsequent score is significantly higher than the earlier, lower score—even if there is no apparent excuse for the disappointing score.

Finally, if you must have a higher score to gain admission, then obviously you must take the test again. You should understand, however, that there is a point after which it just doesn't make sense to take the LSAT again. Even if you happen to have a particularly good day and improve dramatically, your chances for admission may not improve. If a law school admissions officer sees a string of low scores followed by a single good score, the single good score is likely to be regarded as an anomaly and therefore dismissed.

Note: LSAS does not automatically inform law schools that a candidate is planning to take another LSAT. If you determine that it is necessary to retake the test, contact any law schools at which you have applications pending. Explain that you are retaking the test, and ask them to delay taking any unfavorable action on the application until the results of the retesting are available.

LSDAS

LSDAS is an acronym for Law School Data Assembly Service. LSDAS is a central clearing house for information about law school applicants, and almost all ABA-accredited law schools require that you subscribe to the service.

When you register with LSDAS, you will complete computerized forms that summarize basic biographical information such as when you were born, where you went to college, and when you graduated or expect to graduate. It is your responsibility to ask all schools that you have attended to send copies of your academic transcripts to LSDAS. LSDAS then summarizes certain information and forwards the summary and copies of the transcripts along with copies of LSAT results to the schools to which you are applying. (So, you will request only one transcript per school, the one for LSDAS. You won't need to send a separate transcript to every school to which you are applying.)

You will be charged a fee for this service, and the fee will vary according to the number of schools you are applying to and also according to when you request that reports be sent to schools. (Provision is made by LSAS for fee waivers for those candidates who cannot afford the subscription fee.)

An LSDAS subscription is good for one year from the date that it is processed by LSDAS, but you can renew your subscription upon payment of another fee. Since you control the timing of the subscription, select a date for your initial registration so that your subscription covers the application season in which you will be participating. It is administratively easier to register for both the LSAT and the LSDAS at the same time. Thus, if you are taking the mid-winter, late spring, or early fall administration of the LSAT (as suggested above), register for LSDAS when you register to take the test. Your LSDAS subscription will cover the period during which you are submitting applications.

You may have many other questions about LSDAS, but this is not the appropriate forum in which to address them. LSAS gives extensive and very explicit instructions with the LSDAS forms provided in its "Information Bulletin." There are a few features of the LSDAS that are generally relevant to the current task:

You must arrange for transcripts to be forwarded to LSDAS from *every* post-secondary school you have attended. There are even special forms to be filed in case a transcript is no longer available.

Although LSDAS insists upon a complete report, you control the dissemination of that report. It is sent only to those law schools you designate.

LSDAS summarizes only your undergraduate grades—not graduate marks. LSDAS will forward to law schools copies of graduate transcripts, provided that it has those transcripts prior to the summarization of your undergraduate work. Therefore, if you have graduate work that is important to your application, be sure to get the transcript to LSDAS on time.

Grades are converted to a standard 4.0 scale. LSDAS has an elaborate conversion system that takes account of the variations in college transcripts. All of the following and more are governed by some rule:

- Quarter system rather than semester system
- Pass/Fail rather than grades
- Pass/Fail for ROTC, PE, etc., rather than grades
- Numerical rather than letter grades
- Letter grades modified by plus or minus
- Withdrawal both with and without credit

We understand that you may have many other questions about the exact procedures used by LSDAS, but those questions are best answered by LSAS. Read carefully the LSAS "Information Bulletin," and contact LSAS if you have questions. For the present discussion, we can skip those questions and proceed with our discussion.

DEAN'S EVALUATION

This part of the application is very important, but it is easily disposed of. The form might look like that shown on the following page.

COLLEGE DEAN'S EVALUATION FORM

Applicant,

Please provide the following information and give this form to the Dean of Students. (Note: You must have the Dean of Students complete this form regardless of whether that person knows you.)

Your Name   Class

Your Address

Dean's Name

To be completed by the Dean:

1. Has the person named above been found guilty of any academic or other impropriety? If so, please describe.

2. Has the applicant otherwise behaved in a manner inconsistent with the trust and responsibility expected of lawyers? If yes, please explain.

3. Are there any disciplinary charges currently pending against the applicant? If yes, please explain.

4. Would you recommend the applicant for admission to law school?
   I do not know the applicant well enough to answer.
   Yes, very enthusiastically.
   Yes, with conviction.
   Yes, but with qualifications.
   No, I would not recommend the applicant.

Signature:

Notice that the form specifically states that it is the Dean who must execute the form, regardless of whether the Dean knows the applicant personally.

The Dean's Form is very important in the sense that a law school will not process an application without the form. But in most cases its only real function is to elicit any negative information in a college's files that might not otherwise become a part of the application.

LETTERS OF RECOMMENDATION

As part of the application process, many law schools ask that applicants have two or three outside parties send directly to the school letters in which they comment on the applicant's background. Other law schools don't require such letters but accept them if the applicant arranges for them. These letters are often referred to as letters of recommendation.

There are two widely held misconceptions about letters of recommendation. First, many people wrongly believe that the quality of a letter of recommendation is entirely a function of the title of the writer. Mention "letters of recommendation" to these people and they immediately start reviewing a mental list of relatives, family friends, and long-forgotten acquaintances looking for the names of judges, elected officials, and prominent attorneys upon whom they might impose for a letter.

This "star search" approach to choosing people to write letters of recommendation is misguided. Admissions officers are not particularly interested in learning that you are politically or socially well-connected. In fact, the "star search" approach may very well backfire.

One law school admissions officer tells of a letter the school received from the vice-president of the United States. The applicant had evidently met the vice-president at some political rally and had enough clout within the party to get a "letter of recommendation" on the official letterhead of the vice-president of the United States. The gist of the letter follows:

> *To the committee:*
> *I recommend this applicant for admission to your law school. I met the applicant at an official function, and I was very impressed with his honest face and firm handshake.*
> *Sincerely,*
> *Vice-President of the United States*

The letter had the unintended side effect of providing some amusement for the people in the admissions office, but it didn't advance the applicant's cause. In fact, the letter almost certainly hurt the applicant's chances. The applicant seemed to have been thinking, "The vice-president is so important they'll have to accept me." But law school admissions officers don't have to take orders from the vice-president. Those at this school were understandably insulted that the applicant thought them so unsophisticated.

We do not mean to imply that you should avoid obtaining letters of evaluation from prominent people. The fatal flaw in the letter above is not that it was written by the vice-president of the United States. Rather, the problem with the letter is that it says nothing relevent about the applicant. There is no basis for the conclusion that the law school should accept the applicant. Below we will show you how to avoid this error.

There is a second widely held misconception that is, in a way, the mirror image of the "star search" fallacy. It finds voice in the common sentiment, "Don't bother with letters of recommendation. Law schools don't pay attention to them anyway." In fact, there may be a kernel of truth in this view. After all, what weight could be given to the kind of letter described above? Letters like that may explain why some law schools don't seem to be particularly enthusiastic about receiving letters of recommendation: The letters are so superficial and perfunctory that they are of no value whatsoever in evaluating an applicant.

Yet, other law schools do solicit and even insist upon letters of recommendation. Why? Because they know that a well-considered letter of recommendation from an appropriate source can refine their picture of the applicant. For those schools that solicit or require letters of recommendation, it is very important that you make every effort to secure effective letters and that you follow through to be certain that the letters are submitted before the deadline. Since those schools expect to see effective letters, an application without them appears to be defective and may even be disregarded as "incomplete."

Even if a school doesn't require letters of recommendation, you should arrange to have yours sent there. Paradoxically, an effective letter of recommendation may actually be very important at a school that seems less than enthusiastic about such letters. The fact that a school is not very interested in letters of recommendation may say something about the quality of letters that the school usually receives. If, by and large, the letters don't add anything to the admissions process, then you can understand why they don't really want to be burdened with them. On the other hand, imagine that they receive a very powerful letter. Since the other applicants have arranged only for some perfunctory letter or have elected not to solicit any at all, the rare, very powerful letter of recommendation takes on even greater significance. In the same way that an application without effective letters looks defective to a school that requires such letters, at a school that does not require them the application with an effective letter really stands out.

Now that you know that you should arrange for letters of recommendation (even if the school neither encourages nor requires them), we need to discuss the elements that make for an effective letter. To start with, we will discard the phrase "letter of recommendation" and adopt the more accurate description "letter of evaluation." To be sure, you will want to make certain that your letter writers are favorable to your cause and "recommend" you for admission, but an effective letter must go beyond a simple recommendation. An effective letter contains an evaluation of the applicant's qualifications.

A good letter of evaluation has three important features:

1. It shows that the writer is someone who knows enough about intellectual ability and academic or professional effectiveness in general to make comparative judgments about the qualifications of the particular applicant.

2. It shows that the writer is someone who knows enough about the particular applicant to make an informed judgment about the applicant's qualifications.

3. It contains not only the writer's general conclusions about the applicant but enough supporting detail to make those conclusions believable.

Each of these features is essential. As for the first, for the letter to be effective, the writer must be able to contribute some information about those qualities that bear on the applicant's ability to be successful as a law student and later as a lawyer. Obviously, a letter from a lawyer is appropriate. But the writer need not be a lawyer. Also appropriate would be a letter from a college professor, whose job it is to evaluate students. In fact, a good letter of evaluation may come from a person who really doesn't know what qualities are desirable for the study of law. For example, an employer who writes about an applicant's analytical ability and communications skills is providing an admissions committee with important information.

Law schools that require letters of evaluation usually specify that one or more come from college professors. For applicants who are still in college or who have only recently graduated from college, that requirement should not be difficult to satisfy. Applicants who have been out of school for four or five years may worry that it will be difficult to find a professor who is able to write a meaningful letter of evaluation. And for applicants who have been out of college for ten years or more, it may be impossible to find a professor to write a letter of evaluation:

(Telephone conversation between an older applicant and the applicant's alma mater)

Applicant: I'm applying to law school, so I would like to ask Professor Smith of the Economics Department for a letter of evaluation.

Alma Mater: I'm sorry, but when Professor Smith retired last year, she moved to Europe and left no forwarding address.

Applicant: Then I'd like to speak to Professor Jones in the Political Science Department.

Alma Mater: I'm sorry, but two years ago several students implicated Professor Jones in a sex-for-grades scandal, and he disappeared.

Applicant: Well, how about Professor Johnson in the English Department?

Alma Mater: I'm sorry, but Professor Johnson died last year. He's buried in the poet's corner of the University Cemetery.

Applicant: Well I suppose I'll start with Professor Johnson. At least we know where he is.

Law schools are aware of the problems older applicants may encounter in their search for professors. If you are an older applicant, make your best effort to honor the letter of the instructions. But if you cannot find a professor who is able to write a letter on your behalf, find a substitute such as another employment-related letter. It is probably a good idea to attach a note to the application explaining in one or two sentences that your efforts were unsuccessful.

The second requirement for an effective letter of evaluation (that the person writing the letter be familiar with the applicant as an individual) is straightforward. Unless the letter writer has sufficient information on which to base an opinion, the letter simply won't be credible. This requirement is another reason why law schools ask for letters from professors. A college professor may be the person who has the most information about your abilities. You should try to find a professor with whom you have taken two or more courses, that is, someone who is really able to comment meaningfully on your performance. Don't fall into the "star search" trap. Prefer a teacher with whom you have worked closely to the chair of the department with whom you have not worked at all.

If you have significant work experience, you will also want to find a writer who is able to comment on your performance from that perspective. Again, avoid the "star search" error. It is probably better to ask your immediate superior, who is very familiar with your employment record, to write a letter evaluating your professional background than to ask for a letter from the president of the entire company when the president is not really familiar with your abilities.

Sometimes an applicant may be reluctant to ask an employer for a letter of evaluation because the employer doesn't know that the applicant is applying to law school, and the applicant doesn't want the employer to know. If an applicant has significant work experience, law schools will obviously be expecting a letter of evaluation covering that aspect of the applicant's life. The lack of such a letter may cause the admissions officer to draw a negative conclusion: The applicant couldn't find anyone to write a positive letter.

An applicant in the position described above seems to be caught on the horns of a dilemma: Don't provide a letter covering the employment history and allow the admissions officer to draw an adverse conclusion, or inform the boss and jeopardize the position at the firm. There is a way to slip between the horns of the dilemma. If you find yourself in the position described above, use a colleague or an outside business associate as a letter writer.

The person you select for this purpose must satisfy the first requirement of a good letter writer—a basis for comparison. The technician who services the office's computer system may be an electronic wizard, but that alone doesn't qualify the technician to write a letter of evaluation for a law school applicant. But a professional colleague may fit the bill—someone who has professional responsibilities and might be expected to write the same sort of letter for a subordinate. Or you might look outside the firm. A business contact who writes letters of evaluation for employees in another firm can certainly write one for you.

APPLICATION FORM

Although each law school develops its own application form, these forms don't vary much from school to school. All ask for essentially the same information, and there is little you can do to control the content of the application form. On the next two pages, you will find a mock application form that is a composite of several forms from different schools:

STUDENT APPLICATION FORM

(Please print or type.)
Personal Information

Check One: Mr.   Mrs.   Miss   Ms.

Full Name: _____
                    Last   First   Middle

Permanent
Address: _____
                    Number   Street

_____

                    City   State   Zip Code

Date of   Place of   Telephone
Birth: Birth: Number:

Are you a U.S. citizen?   Yes   No

If no, what is your citizenship? _____

Are you a permanent resident of the U.S.?   Yes   No

Academic Background

List all colleges, graduate schools, and professional schools that you
have attended:

Name	Location	Dates		Degree	Date of Grad.
		From	To		
____	____	____	____	___	____	____
____	____	____	____	___	____	____
____	____	____	____	___	____	____

Scholastic Honors:

Extracurricular Activities:

Employment History

All previous employment that is significant:

Dates		Position	Employer and Address	Reason for Leaving
From	To			
———	—	———	———	———
———	—	———	———	———
———	—	———	———	———

Letters of Evaluation

Who will be completing the Candidate Evaluation Form?

(Although only one Candidate Evaluation Form is required, you may wish to submit others.)

Other Information

List all dates on which you have taken or will take the LSAT.

To which other law schools are you applying?

Do you plan to apply for financial aid?

Have you ever been convicted of a crime?

Have you ever been discharged or asked to resign by an employer?

Have you ever applied to this school before?

Have you ever attended another law school?

As you can see, most of your answers are already settled by your background. All you have to do is enter them in the appropriate spaces. A few of the questions, however, merit some comment.

First, what if there is not enough space to list all of your accomplishments or all of your activities? List them on a separate sheet. Just make sure that you label the additional pages clearly and include a reference note on the application form. You may also, if you wish, include a resumé with the application, but the resumé should not be a substitute for answers to the questions on the application form. The admissions people are accustomed to reading their own application forms and expect to see information in the appropriate place.

Second, do you have to answer the question about applying for financial aid? Yes. But don't worry that it will compromise your chances for admission. Most law schools specifically state that need for aid will not affect the admission decision.

Third, why does a law school want to know what other schools you are applying to? We have heard two different theories about this question, but according to both, you don't compromise your chances of admission by answering truthfully. We have been told by one dean that this question is a holdover from times when law schools were competing for applicants, rather than vice versa. So law schools needed the information to know how many candidates to accept to ensure that they would have a full entering class. Another dean tells us that the law schools like to keep track of the "competition." After students have enrolled, they can figure out which candidates matriculated at which schools and plan for the future to attract more and better students. On either theory, you answer to this question should not affect your chance for admission at a school.

Finally, the general rule on all questions is to answer truthfully. Your law school application is your first step for admission to the practice of law. And when the time comes for the final interview before the Moral Fitness Committee of the Board of Bar Examiners, you don't want a misstatement on your law school application coming back to haunt you. If you are in doubt about what is expected of you on a question, call the appropriate admissions office and ask for clarification.

CHAPTER 5

THE PERSONAL STATEMENT

Many law school applications invite you to submit a personal statement in which you may discuss any issue that you think might be relevant to the decision on your application. Some schools even require a personal statement as part of the application. Appropriate topics for the personal statement are background (including family and education), special achievements or experiences, reasons for applying to law school, and professional goals and expectations. The application form may include blank space for the personal statement, or you may be asked to submit the personal statement on a supplemental sheet or sheets.

THE IMPORTANCE OF THE PERSONAL STATEMENT

When asked to name the most important part of the application, many admissions officers answer "the personal statement." This answer will no doubt be cause for excitement for most candidates—consternation for some, relief for others. You must understand the importance of the personal statement in the context of our discussion in Chapter 2. When we analyze the basis of this response of the admissions officers, we find that they mean, "If a candidate is otherwise qualified in terms of GPA and LSAT score, then the personal statement becomes the most important factor in making a final decision on the application." In other words, an effective personal statement can provide an affirmative reason for accepting an application. A persuasive statement may even help a candidate overcome a relatively low GPA or LSAT score. Even a powerful personal statement cannot, however, save an application that is already doomed by a GPA and an LSAT score that are too low.

The personal statement should be the most important part of the application from the point of view of the applicant. The personal statement is the centerpiece of the application surrounded and supported by the LSAT score, the GPA, letters of appraisal, employment history, and lists of achievements. The personal statement gains in significance because it is the one part of the application over which the applicant has short-term control. By the time you begin submitting applications, virtually every aspect of the application other than the personal statement has already been determined. Your GPA is already computed (allowing perhaps for one more semester's grades), your LSAT score is settled (or perhaps pending), and your work record and extracurricular activities are history. The personal statement, however, is yet to be written and so remains under your control. You still have charge of its content, its organization, and its execution.

Despite the importance of the personal statement, we have read countless numbers of them from candidates who apparently believe that the personal statement is one more administrative burden that should be discharged as quickly as possible and with as little effort or inconvenience as possible. The statements written by these candidates reflect this attitude. They are ill-conceived, poorly executed, and they ultimately fail to advance the applicant's case. In fact, a weak personal statement can actually hurt an applicant's chances of acceptance.

Even candidates who understand the importance of the personal statement often fail to achieve maximum advantage from the opportunity it offers. Some fail to keep in mind the factors that admissions officers are looking for and so write statements that are in various ways inappropriate. Others become satisfied with a first or second draft and rest too soon. Drafting and editing a compelling personal statement may take forty or fifty hours or even longer.

We know of one candidate who had already submitted completed applications to two top schools. Even though the applications were already pending, the candidate asked us to read the full submissions and to give our opinion of their effectiveness. After reviewing the application, the candidate's resumé, and the personal statement, we told the candidate that we thought the personal statement failed to achieve maximum effect. The candidate defended the application by explaining that the personal statement had required at least ten hours to complete. But once we pointed out the particular deficiencies of the personal statement, the candidate had to agree with our assessment.

At our suggestion, the candidate immediately contacted the two schools, asked that action on the application be delayed, and arranged to submit substitute applications. Over the next three weeks, we worked at least forty hours by long-distance telephone on the application. The candidate must have invested another forty or fifty hours on top of those spent on the telephone. Finally, the candidate submitted the substitute applications and, we are happy to report, was accepted by both schools.

CONTENT OF THE PERSONAL STATEMENT

We relate the above anecdote in order to stress the importance of making a commitment to writing a meaningful personal statement regardless of the effort required. In this section, we discuss the issues you might address in your personal statement.

Ultimately, the institutional pressures that shape the admissions process will also constrain the content of the personal statement. To be of any value to your application, the points you discuss must bear on one of three general considerations: ability, motivation, or special perspective. (See Chapter 2.) Because your application must show evidence of both ability and motivation, you should first examine it carefully to determine whether there are any weaknesses in it that should be explained.

What would constitute a weakness in an application? A low LSAT score immediately comes to mind. If your LSAT score is significantly below the median LSAT score of the school's recent entering classes, it would be nice to be able to explain that the score is not truly indicative of your ability. Unfortunately, law schools generally have faith in the LSAT score as a predictor of first-year success (even while respecting all of the caveats and disclaimers issued by the test's creators), so it would be difficult to persuade them that the LSAT itself is a defective instrument.

Certainly, if some objective circumstance such as an illness interfered with one taking of the LSAT, and if a subsequent testing resulted in a higher score, then it is probably worth letting the committee know what happened during the first testing. (Some admissions officers suggest that candidates attach a separate statement for such information rather than include it in the personal statement.) It will not do, however, to write in the personal statement, "I just don't do well on tests like the LSAT." If your score is at the bottom of the scale, the admissions committee will already know that you don't do well on the LSAT. Unless there is some concrete reason for a relatively poor LSAT score, then you had probably just better let your higher GPA attest to your academic ability.

On the other hand, given a strong LSAT score, a somewhat disappointing GPA can more easily be explained because the specific causes of a lower GPA are easier to identify: low first year grades due to a "slow start"; a bad semester due to personal illness; a bad semester due to emotional dislocation caused by divorce or death in the family; a generally depressed GPA due to the need to work while a student.

What if both your LSAT score and your GPA are significantly below those typically accepted by the school to which you are applying? Then you might want to reconsider whether it is really worth the application fee to apply to that school. Although it is true that law schools want to accept candidates who are unusual and have something unique to contribute to the school's community, it is not likely that a law school will accept a candidate who cannot in some way demonstrate the ability needed to complete the school's program of study.

If you are satisfied that your application doesn't contain any significant weaknesses, then you should concentrate on developing and emphasizing your strengths. As you study your academic and professional achievements and your community and extracurricular activities, try to get beyond the objective descriptions of those features of your application. Try to understand what those achievements and activities have done for your intellectual and emotional development.

One of the most common mistakes made with the personal statement is simply to repeat in the statement information that is already available to the admissions committee in the application form itself: "I graduated with a 3.5; I got a 150 on the LSAT; I am employed by the bank; and I am a community volunteer." This kind of statement doesn't go beneath the surface of the application.

If you want to discuss items mentioned in the application form, then you should *interpret* your background in such a way that it exhibits the ability or commitment that an admissions committee seeks. You should not merely mention some fact in your personal history. Rather, you should explain to the committee the significance of that fact in determining your decision to apply to law school.

Another common error is to use the personal statement to describe in very vague terms the shortcomings of the legal system and how the applicant will correct all of them once admitted to the bar: "I have always been interested in our system of justice; many poor people and members of minority groups are treated unfairly; as a lawyer, I will represent these groups and redress all the injustices in the world." The chief difficulty with the "save the world" approach is that it usually lacks credibility. If you plan to claim in your personal statement that you want to serve the disenfranchised of our society, then there had better be something in your background such as extensive community service or volunteer work that strongly supports your claim to such a commitment.

In any event, a "noble" purpose is neither a necessary nor a sufficient reason for acceptance at a law school. Although law schools are interested in training some people who will serve the poor, they are also interested in training some lawyers who will earn large fees and contribute money to the school.

Although there is no single preferred content for the personal statement, law school admissions officers do like to be told that their law school holds some special interest for a candidate. So if you have a reason for wanting to attend a particular school, you can include that reason in your personal statement. You might mention, for example, a school's clinical programs or its emphasis on an area such as environmental law. A word of warning: Make sure that your statement is believable. Contrast the following two comments:

I truly want to attend your law school. I was very impressed by Dean Smith's letter in the bulletin in which it is stated that your law school is committed to academic and professional excellence.

Since I plan to become a criminal lawyer, I believe that I would benefit greatly from participation in the law school's legal defense clinical program.

The second statement is believable, while the first sounds contrived.

In addition to the points discussed above, your personal statement will need an overall theme. We know of three formats that have been used with great success over the years. First, you might let motivation be the focus of your statement. Using this format, you would describe the events that have led you to consider the possibility of law school and offer some idea of what you plan to do with a law degree. Remember to be as specific as possible, particularly with regard to the events that prompted you to apply to law school. With regard to the future, you may not be able to be very specific; but if you do already have a position in mind, then mention it.

The "motivation" format for the personal statement is very good for people who have been out of school for a while and whose motivation for going to law school arose gradually through their professional or other activities. Consider some examples:

- A police officer who wants to become a prosecutor or a defense attorney
- An executive at a firm having international contacts who is interested in law as applied to international companies
- A social worker who plans to become an advocate for persons in need of social services
- A financial analyst who wants to work in the area of securities regulation or taxation
- A legal secretary or paralegal who wants to move into the lawyer's office
- An official of a teacher's union with negotiating experience who wants to leave teaching to practice law

We can, for example, imagine the statement of someone who fits the last description. It might read:

I have been a high school teacher and member of the Teacher's Union for twelve years. For six years, I have been actively involved in union business. During our last contract negotiating period, I was a member of the negotiating team. From this experience I learned that I am a skilled negotiator and that I have a facility with legal concepts. Therefore, I now want to go to law school.

This version is, of course, highly abbreviated, but you should be able to see how the general idea could be fleshed out with further details.

A second format that many people use successfully is the "significant experience" format. In this format, the candidate describes an important experience and then draws a moral from the experience. This format is particularly suitable for candidates whose applications establish ability and motivation without the need for further elaboration. For example:

- A graduate of the Peace Corps who describes the work of the Peace Corps in a remote village
- A veteran of the armed forces who retells the story of a humanitarian or perhaps a combat mission
- A member of the Audubon Society who recounts the successful search for a particular species of bird

- An athlete who relates the story of how the championship was won or lost
- A parent who recalls a particularly satisfying or anxious moment during childrearing
- A performer who describes the artistic and personal feelings associated with a performance

Consider a brief sketch of a personal statement submitted to us by a college senior and student of the piano who had been chosen to play one of a series of student concerts with a major orchestra:

> *I was chosen from among 100 pianists after three rounds of competition to play this concert. The piano concerto chosen by the conductor is known as one of the most difficult in the literature. We rehearsed for days and days. At the conclusion of the performance, the audience applauded me enthusiastically, and I acknowledged the applause. Although I have reason to be proud of my accomplishment, on reflection I now understand that my performance almost had to seem good because of the quality of the orchestra. And I now realize that the conductor made sure that the student "star" was presented in the best possible light.*

This particular personal statement does not draw any explicit moral from the experience, although it is possible to infer that it says something about the importance of team work or learning or self-knowledge and so on. With a personal statement of this type, you hope that an admissions officer will say, "This is a very impressive accomplishment, and the writer is a very reflective person—the kind of person who could contribute to our law school class."

The first format described above is suitable, we said, for candidates whose ability is clear from the application form and who want to emphasize motivation. The second format is suitable for those whose ability and motivation are evident in the application form and who want to emphasize their uniqueness. What should you do if you are concerned that either your ability or motivation or both are not obvious from the application form itself?

There is a third format we can recommend: the argument for admission. In this format, a candidate marshalls arguments for admission by using bits of personal history to document ability and motivation. This format is particularly suitable for those candidates whose ability or motivation is not obvious from the application form and for candidates who otherwise just can't decide on what to say in the personal statement. This type of personal statement will have the following structure:

    I. I have the ability to complete law school.
        A. Previous academic study proves this conclusion.
        B. Employment history proves this conclusion.
        C. Extra achievements prove this conclusion.

    II. I am committed to law school.
        A. This is a well-considered decision.
        B. My career plans are formed.

    III. I have something unique to contribute.

Using this format, the personal statement first addresses the issue of the candidate's ability. The first supporting point is intended to show that the candidate's academic record shows the ability to study law, but the personal statement should not simply repeat what is already available to the reader. Rather, the statement should offer additional insights. You might, for example, "recalculate" your GPA by dropping your first year's grades or by using only grades earned in one area of study:

> *My final GPA for all four years of college is lower than it might otherwise have been because of my disappointing freshman year. My GPA for my last three years is 3.65, and for my senior year is 3.8.*

Or:

> *I believe that I am a better student than my 3.4 GPA indicates. My GPA for my major area, which included several demanding courses, is 3.7.*

Or:

> *Although my undergraduate GPA is a bit low, I earned a 3.85 in graduate school and passed all three qualifying exams for my masters degree with Highest Honors.*

You can also offer evidence that the curriculum you designed was very challenging:

Although my major was political science, a quick look at my transcript will show that I took seven courses in philosophy. Had I not wanted to graduate on time, I could have taken another course in philosophy to complete a double major.

Or:

I earned my degree in English Literature in the College's Honors Program. All Honors Program courses require a term paper at least twenty-five pages long.

Or:

Philosophy of Law 402 was taught at the law school for law students, and undergraduates were admitted to the course only with the professor's permission. I was one of only four undergraduates accepted for the seminar and one of only five students to get an A for the course.

The second element of the "ability" contention cites work experience. Here you need to describe the responsibilities you have been given because an admissions officer will not necessarily understand the significance of your position just from the title. We once reviewed an application containing the following entry:

1980–1983   Traffic controller   Union Carbide

To us, the title "Traffic Controller" suggested a person dressed in a uniform with white gloves directing vehicles in and out of the company parking lot. We were wrong. The candidate explained to us that the traffic controller is responsible for making shipping arrangements for hundreds of millions of dollars of freight each year, and further, that the position requires a thorough knowledge of government regulations regarding freight shipments and charges. Moreover, the candidate was the only person to be promoted to such an important position with only four years' experience with the company. When incorporated into the personal statement, the details of the full explanation of the significance of "traffic controller" made the personal statement much more persuasive.

This advice should also be applied to any description of extracurricular or community activities. It is not enough to write, "In 1989, I was chair of the Committee to Save Crandall Park." A fuller explanation is needed:

> In 1989, the city announced that due to fiscal pressures it would close Crandall Park, a 25-acre facility with a swimming pool, a pond, and other recreational facilities situated in a lower-income neighborhood. I organized and was elected chair of the Committee to Save Crandall Park. The Committee got nearly two dozen local merchants to commit over $125,000 in cash and equipment for the preservation of the park. Then the Committee persuaded various civic organizations to take on maintenance tasks such as sweeping and trash collection on a rotating basis. These commitments have been renewed each of the past two years, and the park remains open.

The second major contention of the argument for admission deals with motivation or commitment. You should first try to describe for the admissions committee the considerations that have led you to apply to law school. Then, if possible, look toward the future and indicate what you might do with a law degree. In essence, the second contention of this format will look like an abbreviated version of the first format ("motivation") that we discussed above.

Finally, since admissions officers are trying to create classes that include students with diverse backgrounds and different perspectives, you might comment on any unusual aspect of your background. For example:

> One of my parents is originally from Greece and the other from Puerto Rico. From my relatives I have learned to speak both Greek and Spanish and have been taught to appreciate both the Greek and the Puerto Rican cultures.

WRITING THE STATEMENT

As we noted above, writing the personal statement is not an easy task nor one that can be executed overnight. You should begin by considering carefully what it is you want to say and then organizing those thoughts into a coherent whole. Only then will you be ready to start writing. Initially, you should write the personal statement without regard to length. Be profligate with your words. Then edit the statement carefully with regard to style, grammar, and length.

Your writing style is, of course, your own and is already well-established, but there are some general points you should keep in mind as you write your personal statement. First, don't adorn the statement with legal words or phrases. Admissions officers with whom we have spoken are very clear on this point. Language such as "pursuant to," "aforementioned," and "party" (to mean person) has no place in a personal statement. An attempt to dress up the statement in "legalese" is not likely to impress an admissions officer. Instead, most seem to regard such attempts as unsophisticated and even pathetic.

Second, you should avoid generally the temptation to dress up the statement with large words in an attempt to sound erudite. Consider some sentences from a personal statement we were asked to review:

> *I have always maintained a great interest in our jurispruden-tial system and have always had the propensity to obtain a legal education. However, due to several personal misfortunes in my household, I have not had the opportunity to apply for and attend law school until the present time.*
>
> *I am convinced my personal and professional background would add immeasurably to the school's diversity and firmly believe that my demonstrated graduate academic successes are much more indicative of my scholastic capabilities than the undergraduate work I completed three years ago. Those successes, in conjunction with my LSAT score and my pertinent work experience, should make me an ideal candidate.*

Jurisprudential? Propensity? Personal misfortunes? Household? Scholastic capabilities? Pertinent? The language is strained and makes the writer sound pompous and insincere. You'll fare better if you just express your thoughts directly and in your own words.

Third, avoid the temptation to overstate your case. Again, we refer to the sentences immediately above. This statement asserts that the candidate has *always* been interested in law. Always? Even before kindergarten? And the statement claims that the applicant is an *ideal* candidate who would contribute *immeasurably* to the school. Ideal, as in perfect? And a contribution that can't even be measured?

Don't try to defend the writer by arguing that we are nitpicking. Obviously, the writer meant "for a long time" rather than "always" and "strong candidate with an interesting background" rather than "ideal candidate who would contribute immeasurably." But it is a very strange defense of a law school applicant to say that the personal statement doesn't really say what the applicant intended. After all, lawyers are supposed to choose their words carefully. Using "always" to mean "for a long time" and "ideal" and "immeasurably" to mean "strong" and "significantly" suggests sloppy habits of thought, and sloppy thinking is not desirable in a lawyer.

Grammar

You will obviously want to make sure that your personal statement is free of grammatical mistakes and other errors of expression. Here is a checklist that will help you avoid errors that all too often remain in personal statements even after editing.

1. For every clause, identify the subject and the verb, and make sure that they agree. Modifiers that separate the verb from the subject can obscure a problem of agreement:

   The lawyers in a government agency such as the Equal Employment Opportunity Commission has the power to effect positive social change.

   A law school that offers several clinical programs are particularly attractive since I plan to start my own practice immediately after I am admitted to the bar.

In both sentences, there is a failure of agreement between subject and verb:

lawyers . . . has

school . . . are

The plausibility of the incorrect verb choice, and therefore the chance that the error will go unnoticed, is strengthened by a word or phrase near the verb that might be mistaken for the subject:

Commission has

programs are

You can avoid this type of error by isolating each subject and verb and checking for agreement.

2. Isolate each pronoun used in the personal statement, and make sure that it has a referent to which it clearly refers and with which it agrees. First, a pronoun is used as a substitute for a noun. The noun it replaces is called its antecedent or referent. With the exception of certain idioms such as "*It* is raining," a pronoun that does not have a referent is used incorrectly:

As a freshman, I was not a very serious student, and because of it my overall average is not as high as it might otherwise have been.

Many segments of our society do not have access to adequate legal representation, which is what I plan to help remedy.

In the first sentence, the pronoun "it" lacks a referent. "It" needs to refer to something like "poor freshman year," but there is no such noun in the sentence. The sentence needs to be rewritten:

As a freshman, I was not a very serious student, and because of my poor first-year grades, my overall average is lower than it might otherwise have been.

In the second sentence, the relative pronoun "which" lacks a referent. "Which" seems to refer to something like "problem" or "situation," but no such word appears in the sentence. Use a noun:

Many segments of our society do not have access to adequate legal representation, and the lack of representation is a problem that I plan to help remedy.

Additionally, a pronoun must agree with its referent in number:

For many years, a lawyer was likely to be a white, Anglo-Saxon, Protestant male, but today they come from all types of backgrounds.

The pronoun "they" refers to "lawyer," and the pronoun is plural while the noun is singular. The sentence can be corrected by making the noun plural:

For many years, lawyers were mostly white, Anglo-Saxon, Protestant males, but today they come from all types of backgrounds.

3. Make sure that the elements of a sentence that perform similar or equal functions are presented in parallel form:

At most colleges, the dominant attitude among students is that gaining admission to professional graduate school is more important than to obtain a well-rounded education.

The newspaper's review of my film was very favorable, citing the unusual photography, the complex plot, and the dialogue was very interesting.

In the first sentence, "gaining admission" and "to obtain" must both have the same form: "gaining admission is more important than obtaining." In the second sentence, each element in the series of features should have the same form: "citing the unusual photograph, the complex plot, and the interesting dialogue."

4. Another error to avoid is incomplete construction:

The committee's investigation revealed that the Department Head not only knew but encouraged the policy of using graduate assistants to grade final exams.

I have in the past and will in the future be an advocate for stronger laws to protect our wilderness areas.

For some people, earning a top salary is as important, if not more important than, making a contribution to society.

In each of these sentences, there is an error involving a split construction. In the first sentence, there is a missing preposition. The Department Head did not know the policy itself, rather the Department Head knew *of* the policy: "not only knew of but encouraged . . . ." In the second sentence, the error is in the verb. The auxiliary verb "have" needs the verb "been," but "been" does not appear in the sentence. The sentence can be corrected by completing the construction: ". . . have in the past been and in the future will be . . . ." In the third sentence, the error is an incomplete comparison. The sentence should read ". . . as important *as*, if not more important than . . . ."

5. Make sure that your sentences say what you intend for them to say:

The average salary of a top government official is much lower than the top-level management of most private corporations.

This sentence is guilty of an illogical comparison because it attempts to compare money and people: salary is lower than management. The sentence actually means to compare one salary with another: ". . . is lower than that of the top-level management . . . ."

Another error that we see with some frequency is the infamous dangling modifier:

> *Having just completed a graduate degree in biology, environmental law offers me the best opportunity for professional advancement.*

The sentence as written implies that environmental law has just completed a graduate degree in biology. The sentence must be rewritten:

> *Because I have just completed a graduate degree in biology, environmental law offers me the best opportunity for professional advancement.*

Here is one final example of illogical expression:

> *I received the Fuller Scholarship because my score on the qualifying exam was higher than that of any applicant.*

This sentence makes the illogical assertion that the writer's score was higher than every score—including itself. The proper comparison would be:

> *I received the Fuller Scholarship because my score on the qualifying exam was higher than that of any other applicant.*

6. Finally, do not split an infinitive:

> *Because I know how to efficiently use time, I will be able to successfully complete law school.*

The sentence should be rewritten:

> *"Because I know how to use time efficiently, I will be able to complete law school successfully."*

Editing for Length

The initial draft of your personal statement can be as long as you care to make it, but the final version had better be no longer than two double-spaced, typed pages. For most applicants, a well-edited personal statement doesn't even run a full two pages.

As you edit for length, you will have to make choices about the content of the statement and decisions about the language used. Regarding content, the editing process will force you to jettison some material. You must consciously ask yourself, "Does this point really carry very much weight?" If the answer is "no," then you should delete it and close the gap. With regard to language, you must consciously ask yourself, "Do I really need this word?" If the answer is "no," then delete it.

Editing for length is exacting detail work. Consider an example:

> *My spouse and I have decided to move from New York and relocate to the Los Angeles area. We hold the opinion that California is the region of the country where we want to raise our family and where we both will be able to realize our professional goals and aspirations.*

Does this statement really need the following?

> *"to move from New York and"*
> *"We hold the opinion that"*
> *"the region of the country"*
> *"and aspirations"*

Those words can be deleted without sacrificing any of the content of the paragraph:

> *My spouse and I have decided to relocate to the Los Angeles area. California is where we want to raise our family and where we both will be able to realize our professional goals.*

Sample Personal Statements

In this section, we try to show you the metamorphosis that a personal statement must undergo before it is finally submitted to a law school. For each of three examples, we show a draft version followed by some critical comments. After the critical comments, you will find a final version.

As you study these examples, keep three points in mind. One, the final versions may not be perfect, but they are considerable improvements over the drafts. Two, although we show just two versions, these personal statements actually underwent several revisions. Three, try to notice the subtle changes in style and grammar that were made between the drafts and final versions.

PERSONAL STATEMENT 1—DRAFT

The study and practice of law is challenging, exciting, and directly relevant to my future ambitions. In the next few paragraphs, I intend to explain and justify my belief that I would contribute to the learning environment and diversity of the law school's student body.

I grew up, as one of nine children, on a dairy farm in Fort Ann, a small town in upstate New York. My parents taught their children the value of self-discipline, hard work, and personal initiative. I excelled academically in high school ranking 8/57 and qualified as a Regent's Scholar, Who's Who, and other academic awards.

I attended a nationally acclaimed engineering school at Georgia Tech. While attending this university I worked between 20 and 25 hours each week to support myself. I graduated with an electrical engineering degree while paying for 100% of my education and living expenses. Though my undergraduate record is not outstanding, my grades do show a rising trend during my last two years. I was also able to make the dean's list one semester during which I decreased external hours of employment.

Since I graduated from college, I have been employed in the Nuclear Power Division of the Union Power Company. In my position of employment, I have gained broad experience in the areas of engineering, personnel, and finance and have been promoted to positions of increasingly higher levels of responsibility. I have had experience in managing large projects from design to implementation. I have moved out of the strictly technical career path followed by many engineers to take promotions in the areas of personnel and management.

I currently represent Union Power Company in a joint venture undertaken by 15 utilities with nuclear power plants to create a national employee database for the nuclear industry to draw upon. As committee chairman, I am responsible for the implementation of a significant portion of the system. My duties include

responding to legal concerns dealing with personnel
law.

I also use my employment to enhance my public
speaking and writing abilities. Recently, I was chosen
to participate in a company video training program,
and I have also made presentations at many
management training seminars and have published
articles in company newsletters. As head of the
inter-departmental Quality and Productivity team, I
have found ways to improve the efficiency and
effectiveness of many company programs. As one of the
more respected and successful teams within the
company, we have several times been recognized by the
company with achievement awards. Developing new
programs that require the coordination of personnel
from diverse fields is exhilarating and has required
persistence, organization, and motivation.

Another indication of my motivation and persistence
is my graduate degree. I have just completed an MBA
by attending school in the evenings. My performance in
this program portends future academic success in law
school. I graduated from this quality MBA program
with a GPA of 3.84 and ranked ninth out of 81
graduates. Education for me has and will continue to be
a never-ending goal. While in the MBA program, I
sharpened my analytical and research skills. One of the
research projects I worked on is potentially going to be
published in a financial research journal.

To be well-rounded, it is not only important to
consider yourself and your career but also the needs of
the community. I am involved with a number of civic
organizations that have promoted social good. These
include the Citizens Committee on Poverty of Cowetta
County, in which I hold the position of Treasurer of the
Board of Directors.

During my employment at Union Power, I have
developed admiration for the utility industry and an
awareness of its needs. It is my experience that one of
the major needs of the industry is for quality legal
representation. There are many societal dilemmas that
impact the utility and especially the nuclear industry.
These dilemmas include: (1) The question of nuclear
safety and the growing need for power, (2) The
question of the need for a highly trained work force

and the effects of new legislation on employment practices, and (3) The international versus parochial concerns of the industry. As a lawyer, I could contribute to the advancement of law within these areas.

The diverse curriculum at the law school provides the training necessary to make a contribution toward solving the complex legal problems associated with the utility industry.

Critique

This personal statement needs considerable editing. The primary weakness of the statement is its lack of any overall organizing theme. The first half of the statement follows a chronological order, but then the chronology breaks down and points seem strung together in no particular order. Because the points are not arranged around a theme such as ability or motivation, the potential persuasive effect of the statement is never fully realized.

Additionally, the statement is at least twice as long as it needs to be. Even when the statement makes points that are important, the language is needlessly wordy and awkward. And the statement includes irrelevant information and information that, while relevant, is already included in the application form. The problem of length is at least partially a result of the lack of organization. If a statement lacks a guiding theme, there is a strong temptation to toss in any point that seems interesting.

This statement should be reorganized into a "motivation" statement, the first format discussed above. We have here a candidate whose considerable professional accomplishments can be presented in the application form and on a resume without the need for extensive explanation. The drift in professional development away from technical positions to managerial positions fits naturally into the "motivation" format.

We will begin by eliminating most of the first three paragraphs. The praise of law as challenging and exciting is gratuitous, and the candidate's high school achievements are no longer relevant. From the third paragraph, we will salvage the point about working part-time as an undergraduate.

From the rest of the essay, we will take three points:

Description of the writer's career path
Description of responsibilities assumed
Importance of MBA studies

We will try to weave these strands together in a statement that shows the candidate's reason for applying to law school.

We will discard the paragraph on community work because it is too wordy and because that information also appears in the standard application form. Repeating it here adds nothing to the application.

Finally, we will seize on the paragraph regarding the dilemmas presented by nuclear power to show what the candidate will do with a law degree. In essence, the statement will say, "Here is a candidate with considerable professional accomplishments who wants a law degree for a specific reason."

PERSONAL STATEMENT 1—FINAL VERSION

Since my graduation from college, I have worked for the Nuclear Power Division of Union Power Company. Because my undergraduate degree was in electrical engineering, I initially entered upon a technical career path with Union Power. Over the past ten years, however, I have moved steadily away from the technical side of the industry toward the personnel and management side.

As my resumé shows, with each move I have been given increasingly important responsibilities in these areas. My present assignment is to represent Union Power in a joint venture that includes fifteen nuclear utilities. The objective of the venture is to develop a national employee database for the nuclear industry to draw upon. As committee chair, I am responsible for the implementation of a significant part of the system. One of my duties is to ensure that the system does not lead to unfair or illegal employment practices.

I have just received an MBA degree, and I view a J.D. degree as the completion of a gradual transition from the technical side of the nuclear power industry to the management side of the industry. Managers in the nuclear power industry confront a number of problems: the question of nuclear safety and the growing need for power; the question of the need for a highly trained work force and the effects of new legislation on employment practices; and the need to assess regional needs in light of national policy and international concerns. As a lawyer, I will be in a better position to help the nuclear power industry resolve these issues.

I understand that my college GPA is somewhat low. I would point out that I was one of nine children raised on a dairy farm in rural New York, so it was necessary for me to work my way through school. By working 20 to 25 hours each week during the academic year, I graduated from college with absolutely no indebtedness. I believe that my performance in the MBA program is a better indicator of my academic ability than my college GPA. Also, I was recently chosen to participate in a company video training program. I have enclosed a brief excerpt of my participation in the program so the committee might assess my ability as a speaker.

PERSONAL STATEMENT 2—DRAFT

Upon arriving, the blaze was still dancing up the side of the old tenement building. I located the former residents of this now burned out shell to gather information, which I would later utilize in determining the cause and origin of the fire. As I spoke to them, I could see the pain of their losses etched into their faces. The only consolation I could offer them myself was that they had all managed to survive the disaster.

The subsequent investigation led to my uncovering the source of the fire. A young man, hired by the owner of the building, had set the blaze. Although this was only one of hundreds of such crimes I had investigated, my mind was filled with the unanswered questions: What will happen to the victims of this crime? Where will they go? Who will help them? I realized more had to be done.

Since 1982, I have been employed as a Fire Marshal with the City Fire Department. I know that in my position with the Department, my ability to help people is limited in scope. I believe as an attorney, I will be able to reach out and provide assistance with a far greater sphere of influence.

Throughout my years of employment with the Fire Department, I have gained exposure to criminal law as well as civil and criminal court proceedings. I have often been present in criminal and civil courts and have witnessed the problems that the lower socio-economic population faces in interacting with attorneys and the court system. As a Mexican-American, I possess an in-depth understanding of the culture of the Mexican community. I believe the lower socio-economic and minority populations are often inadequately served by their attorneys, who are frequently unable to understand the needs of these people. Being thoroughly bilingual, I believe I will be a strong asset in assisting this population.

From 1978 through 1982, I completed a bachelor's degree in Fire Service Administration. It was my desire to immediately continue on with my studies by entering law school. But I also had two children, who at this time, were in need of financial assistance for their educations. It was my decision at that time to forgo my studies until my children had completed their training.

I am now at a point in both my career and personal life which will enable me to devote my energies to pursuing my study of law. I believe I possess a unique background which will allow me to be an effective attorney and thus be able to advocate for these people of the community, which I believe have long been underserved.

Critique

Our main criticism of this statement is that it fails to maximize the writer's opportunities. The writer never follows through on the dramatic impact created by the images of the first paragraphs. Additionally, the writer fails to use an excellent opportunity to address the issue of ability.

First, the statement seems to combine two incomplete lines of thought. Consider the initial development:

> *Paragraph 1: The building burned, and I couldn't help the people who had lost their homes.*
> *Paragraph 2: As is often the case, the tenants are the victims of arson.*

Paragraph 3: As Fire Marshal my ability to help is limited. As an attorney, I will be able to do more.

What we would expect at this point is a statement of how the writer hopes to help the people described in the first two paragraphs. Instead, paragraph four falls into the error we cautioned against of making a general indictment of the legal system followed by a promise to make everything better.

To be sure, the second half of the fourth paragraph gives an excellent reason to train the writer as a lawyer: the writer is bilingual and is familiar with Mexican culture. But the lack of a connection between the people described in the first two paragraphs and those referred to generally in the fourth paragraph leaves us wondering what the writer plans to do as a lawyer.

Second, the writer misses a golden opportunity to discuss the issue of ability. The writer is an investigator, and surely the skills of an investigator—attention to detail and systematic thinking—would serve the candidate well in law school.

Finally, the fifth paragraph seems to us a little disingenuous. The writer seems to be telling us that the degree in Fire Service Administration was intended to be preparation for law school. It might very well be that the writer did intend to go to law school upon graduation from college, but the statement reads as though that part might have been concocted for the benefit of the reader.

This personal statement can be strengthened by adding detail and by weaving more closely together the various strands of thought. The final statement does this.

PERSONAL STATEMENT 2—FINAL VERSION

When I arrived at 3 a.m. that January night, the blaze still danced up the side of the old tenement building. I located the former residents of this now burned-out shell to gather information, which I would later use in determining the cause of the fire. As I spoke to them, I could see the pain of their losses etched into their faces. The only consolation I could offer was that they had all managed to survive the disaster.

My subsequent investigation uncovered the source of the fire: arson. I interviewed the former tenants, most

of whom are Mexican-American and speak only
Spanish or at least prefer to speak Spanish. With their
assistance, I identified the arsonist, a young man who
eventually confessed that the owner of the building had
hired him to set the blaze. I have attached a copy of the
newspaper account of this crime to this personal
statement.

Since 1982, I have been a Fire Marshal with the City
Fire Department, and during this time I have
investigated hundreds of cases. Not all cases are so
easily solved. An investigator must gather many pieces
of seemingly unimportant information, and the process
of gathering the facts can be lengthy and tedious. Then,
the facts must be systematically organized to create a
picture of the crime. Creating a picture of a crime is an
act of creative imagination, but it is important to avoid
unwarranted deductions. A false assumption or a
conclusion too hastily drawn can be fatal to an
investigation.

Through my employment, I have been exposed to
both criminal and civil proceedings, and on many
occasions, I have thought of applying to law school. For
years, family responsibilities (a spouse and two
children) made law school impossible. Now that my
children are nearly grown, it is possible for me finally
to apply to law school.

My fluency in Spanish and the skills I have developed
as an investigator should help me become a good
lawyer. I have discussed the decision to apply to law
school with the prosecutors I often work with, and
they think I might make a good prosecuting attorney.

PERSONAL STATEMENT 3—DRAFT

I have chosen your law school because of the
noted specialty it offers in international law as the
place where I would most like to receive my legal
education. My ability to succeed is illustrated by my
academic record and challenging curriculum as an
undergraduate at the University's School of
International Studies, my strong research and
communications skills at various selected internships

and employment, as well as by my dedication to the University's community.

This May, I will graduate with a 3.7 grade point average in my major, International Politics, from the David Thorpe School of International Studies. I received Dean's list honors my last two years as I chose courses that interested me in the field of International Politics such as International Law, Crises in South American Relations, and Political Geography. I also passed the required Oral Spanish Proficiency examination which tested not only my fluency and command of the Spanish language but also my knowledge of Spain and Latin America in the areas of politics, economics, and history. Despite my average LSAT score, I believe my academic honors and my challenging curriculum show that I have the ability to face the rigorous caseloads and demands expected at the law school.

My courses in my major required extensive research, and I became confident in writing large term papers each semester. Being on the East Coast, it was possible to travel to Washington, D.C., to do firsthand research by personally communicating with foreign embassies, American and foreign businesses, and international organizations. I learned to find and cultivate primary sources in addition to secondary sources. These research skills are necessary for law school. The government documents I closely examined on CIA covert action in Latin America for my paper, "The Effect of Hierarchical Organization on Intelligence Agencies: The Decision to Support the Invasion of Cuba," are similar to the shepardizing of cases and the scrutinizing of existing statutes that I must be able to do in law school.

My various internships demanded research also. I spent one summer interning for the National Journalism Center in an academically accredited program. I gathered materials on airline deregulation at the Library of Congress and various Senate Committee offices. My research culminated in my drafting a paper on airline deregulation and contributing to a series of articles appearing in The Tribune. This research experience should be a significant help to me for the preparation required for law school papers and briefs.

Interning for Martin, Collier and Taft (an International Law firm) my senior year of college, I worked exclusively for a partner who was one of my professors at the university. I prepared published reports for the firm's clients. In these reports, I analyzed the issues, developments, and implications for United States businessmen on what to expect from the emergence of the European Common Market. I also drafted and edited articles for the firm's client newsletter on the new federal government legislation dealing with international cases of commerce and trade. Interpreting and explaining in laymen's terms these complex legal issues has helped me to familiarize myself with the legal terminology as well as to prepare me for handling complicated fact situations which I will have to confront in law school.

Wanting to give something back to the student community, I joined the Women's Caucus. During my senior year, as vice-president of the organization, I organized and led a campaign to secure university financing for on-campus childcare for the families of university employees. The facility now provides full-time child care for twenty children. I believe that this experience strengthened my commitment to family values.

Continuing my desire to hold a leadership position, I became active in the student body at the University. I was chosen as a class representative my junior and senior years and planned special events and organized various class committees. I had to allocate my time carefully to handle my challenging schedule, and I believe this self-discipline is the key to success in law school.

Law has always been a part of my life, and my familiarity with law began when my father would return home from his own general law practice and describe the various cases and legal situations that he had encountered for that day. My interest in international relations led me to take courses in international law, and I became curious in learning more about the field. My internship at the International Law firm and my friendship with one of the partners furthered my desire to learn more.

Critique

Let's begin this critique with a question: Were you able to read the entire statement? We managed—but only with great difficulty and, quite frankly, because we had to. This is the classic "over-achiever" personal statement. (Being an "over-achiever" is not necessarily bad, but writing a statement about yourself that is too long is not good.) This statement is afflicted with several serious weaknesses that are all too common.

First, it's too "busy." Some events in your life are more important than others, and you will have to choose to highlight some and ignore others.

Second, the statement is not organized around a central theme. It is simply a series of anecdotes strung together, punctuated by conclusions about what might be valuable for the study of law.

Third, it's "preachy." The writer keeps telling the law school admissions officer what skills are needed for the study of law. But law school admissions officers already know what skills they are looking for. The personal statement should exhibit the skills and leave it to the admissions officers to draw the appropriate conclusions. In fact, if we delete every sentence that explains what the admissions officer should be looking for, we will already shorten the statement considerably. Even so, we need to trim a lot of excess verbiage.

Finally, the statement repeats a lot of information already included in the application form. For example, the writer doesn't need to repeat the name "David Thorpe School of International Studies" or the name of the law firm. Both are clearly identified for the committee in the application form.

The final version of this statement is the result of considerable editing.

PERSONAL STATEMENT 3—FINAL VERSION

I am applying to your law school because I want to pursue a career in international law. Next semester, I will graduate with at least a 3.7 grade point average in my major, International Politics, and I have already passed the department's Oral Proficiency Exam in Spanish. The exam tests not only fluency in Spanish but also knowledge of the politics, economics, and history of Spain and Latin America. The two most important skills I have acquired from my studies and internships are the ability to do research and the ability to write clearly.

Most of the courses in the Department of International Politics require at least one major paper on a topic approved in advance by the professor, and the department's professors encourage students to research a narrow question in depth rather than to write generally and superficially about some large event. Thus, I learned to burrow deeply into the library to find the transcript of a hearing held by some obscure Congressional subcommittee or an editorial in a Spanish language newspaper. To give the committee a better idea of the scope of research required by these courses I have enclosed a copy of the introduction to and the bibliography for a paper I wrote entitled "The Effect of Hierarchical Organization on Intelligence Agencies: The Decision to Support the Invasion of Cuba." For other projects, I traveled to Washington, D.C., where I visited foreign embassies and international organizations and interviewed American and foreign businesses.

Both my internships (summer at the National Journalism Center and my senior year at a firm specializing in international law) required extensive research and writing, but there I concentrated on economic and business questions rather than the issues of foreign policy studied in college. At the National Journalism Center, I contributed to a series of articles on airline deregulation published in The Tribune. At the law firm, I concentrated on the implications for U.S. business of the emergence of the European Common Market. I also drafted and edited articles for the firm's client newsletter on new federal legislation on commerce and trade.

Finally, I would mention that I was for three years a member of the Women's Caucus. As the organization's vice-president my senior year, I organized and led a campaign to secure university funding for on-campus childcare for the families of university employees. This facility now provides full-time childcare for twenty children.

CHAPTER **6**

PREPARING TO TAKE THE LSAT

As we pointed out in Chapter 2, your LSAT score, which is the result of a test only a half-day long, may very well count for as much in your application as the GPA it took you four years to earn. Clearly, you want to do your very best on the LSAT. In this chapter we take up the question of how to prepare for the LSAT and provide some sample preparation materials to help you get started.

LSAT PREPARATION

Basically, there are two methods of preparing for the LSAT: independent study and coaching programs. Either approach can be effective. We will discuss some important features of each method so that you will be in a position to make an informed decision as you get ready to take the exam. We will first discuss the independent study option.

Many people prepare for the LSAT on their own using just written materials. Generally, written test preparation materials come from one of two sources: Law Services or book publishers such as ARCO. The LSAT/LSDAS registration bulletin available from Law Services provides some material designed to familiarize registrants with the content of the LSAT. Additionally, it is possible to purchase from Law Services copies of previously administered LSAT questions. The disadvantage of using only materials distributed by Law Services is that they do not provide a systematic and comprehensive treatment of the test. They are intended to familiarize registrants with the LSAT, but they do not constitute a *course* of preparation for the exam.

ARCO publishes an LSAT study guide entitled *SuperCourse for the LSAT*, which is a complete self-study course of preparation for the LSAT. Its instructional chapters review the patterns of the LSAT and teach strategies for attacking LSAT problems. The book also contains practice material that is equivalent in length to ten actual exams.

Additionally, ARCO publishes a practice handbook entitled *Preparation for the LSAT*.

The other approach to LSAT preparation is to take a course—if one is available in your area. Traditionally, such courses have been offered by private companies, but they are becoming increasingly available at colleges and universities through their continuing education or extension divisions. Live coaching courses usually offer twenty to forty hours of classroom instruction plus some homestudy materials.

Many people who opt to take a live course mention favorably the discipline imposed on students by a live course. They report to us that the regularly scheduled classes and homework assignments force them to do work they might otherwise neglect if they were studying on their own. The primary disadvantage of the live preparation courses offered by most private companies is the cost, which is almost always several hundred dollars.

If you decide to enroll in a course of live instruction, evaluate carefully the advertising claims made about the course, especially those regarding course content, score improvements, and guarantees. Sometimes these claims are misleading.

First, you should understand that preparing for the LSAT is not like preparing for an ordinary college exam. The final exam in a typical college survey course such as European History Since 1600 or Introduction to Psychology tests mastery of certain concepts covered in a clearly defined body of material. This mastery can be achieved in a relatively short period of time by studying the assigned text, and the more facts you memorize, the better you are likely to do on the test.

The LSAT, however, tests reading and reasoning skills that are acquired over a fairly long period—not discrete facts memorized for a particular exam. An LSAT coaching course, which typically lasts only a few weeks, is not likely to improve dramatically your basic reading and reasoning skills. Rather, a good LSAT preparation course will help you sharpen those skills by prompting you to read and to reason more carefully than you usually do. Additionally, a good LSAT course will familiarize you with common question types and teach you strategies for handling those questions.

Since the LSAT tests skills rather than knowledge of facts, lengthy study of the memorizing sort is not likely to improve your LSAT score. Yet, we have known many people who have enrolled in one or another test preparation course because the course offered "hundreds of hours" of instruction. In our experience, few people ever use "hundreds of hours" of instruction, and we doubt that doing an endless succession of practice questions has any real value.

Furthermore, you should view with heightened skepticism any claim that a course will teach you "tricks" that will allow you to "beat" the test. LSAT problems must be solved by reading and reasoning carefully. While familiarity and practice can improve the skills tested by the LSAT, ultimately there is no substitute for careful thinking.

Second, you should be wary of any claim regarding "average score improvement" because score results can be easily manipulated. Some private companies accomplish this by setting up an "internal study." The "internal study" compares student scores on a pre-test administered at the beginning of the course with student scores on a exit-test administered at the end of the course.

In order to obtain very impressive "score improvements," the "internal study" uses a very difficult pre-test on which students perform poorly and a very easy exit-test on which students perform very well. The study will show a tremendous "average score improvement," but the seeming improvement in test scores is attributable to the design of the study rather than to any real improvement in the skills of the student population.

Finally, study carefully the terms of any "guarantee" offered by a course. Common sense dictates that no one can guarantee results in an undertaking of this sort, so most so-called guarantees really just allow students who are dissatisfied with their test results to take a course a second time. In our experience, sitting through a preparation course a second time is not usually very helpful.

In issuing these warnings, we do not wish to discourage you from taking a live test preparation course. Although courses can be expensive, even small differences in LSAT scores can be important. As one admissions officer told us, "We rejected several students with LSAT scores of 150 who would have been accepted had they had 155 or better." Yes, test preparation costs money, but it is money invested in a professional career.

One way of controlling the cost of preparing for the LSAT is to buy cautiously. You may want to start by using the study guides published by ARCO. Then, if you determine that you want to take a live test preparation course, shop around. You may find that a course offered by the extension division of a college or university is considerably less expensive than one offered by a private company.

THE FORMAT OF THE LSAT

The LSAT is a multiple-choice, machine-scored exam that covers three topics: Analytical Reasoning (logical puzzles and games), Logical

Reasoning (analysis of verbal arguments), and Reading Comprehension (questions based on reading selections). Additionally, you will be required to write an impromptu essay on a surprise topic. This writing sample is not scored, but copies of your essay will be sent to all law schools that you have designated to receive copies of your LSAT score report.

The LSAT consists of five separately timed sections, each with a time limit of thirty-five minutes. The time limit for the writing sample, which is usually administered last, is thirty minutes. During the test, you are allowed to work only on the section that is being timed. You may not go back to sections that were previously completed, nor are you permitted to skip ahead. The exam proctor announces when time for work on a section begins and when it ends.

The number of questions in a section depends on the topic tested:

Question Type	Usual Number of Questions
Analytical Reasoning	22–24
Logical Reasoning	24–26
Reading Comprehension	26–28

The test as a whole will include one Analytical Reasoning section, two Logical Reasoning sections, one Reading Comprehension section, plus one "wild card" section. The "wild card" section may test any of the three LSAT topics, but it will not be scored. The "wild card" section contains questions that are still in a developmental phase during which their suitability for use on a future test is under study. Your LSAT might look like this:

Section	Topic	Number of Questions	Time Limit
1	Reading Comprehension	27	35 min.
2	Logical Reasoning	25	35 min.
3	Analytical Reasoning	24	35 min.
4	Logical Reasoning	26	35 min.
5	Reading Comprehension	28	35 min.
Writing Sample			30 min.

Notice that this test form uses two sections of Reading Comprehension. Only one of them would be scored; the other would be the "wild card" section—though test-takers would not know which is which during the administration of the exam. Only after the test results are released would it be possible to determine which Reading Comprehension section was "live" and which was the "wild card."

SCORING THE LSAT

You enter your answers to questions on an answer sheet by blackening appropriate spaces on a grid. This answer sheet is machine graded, and a computer generates your LSAT score. Your score will be reported on a three-digit scale ranging from 120 (the lowest possible score) to 180 (the highest possible score). This scaled score is a function of the raw score, and the raw score is simply the number of questions you answer correctly. Incorrect answers and omissions are not used in computing the score. In other words, there is no penalty on the LSAT for a missed question.

GENERAL ATTACK STRATEGIES

Although the LSAT uses three different topics, there are some methods of attack that are generally applicable to the test as a whole. First, before you begin work on a section, take a few seconds to preview the contents of that section. The preview will remind you of the format of that section and give you an opportunity to recall the important strategies for that type of question.

Additionally, you should be familiar with the instructions for each question type before you go into the exam. No additional time is given during a section for reading the directions, so time spent reading directions is time lost for answering questions.

Pacing is also important. Although the LSAT places a premium on careful reading and analysis, you also have to work within a time limit. You can't afford to work so slowly that you don't get to many of the questions. On the other hand, you can't afford to work so quickly that you make careless errors. Through practice you will find the best compromise between speed and accuracy.

One aspect of effective pacing is knowing when to leave a question. Some LSAT questions are more difficult than others, but all questions are given equal weight in the scoring. No extra credit is given for a difficult question. So you cannot afford to keep working on a question after you have made a reasonable but unsuccessful attempt at a solution. Rather, you should make your guess and keep working through the section.

We just mentioned guessing. Because there is no penalty for an incorrect answer choice, you should answer every question on the test, even those you don't have time to get to. Since there are only five answer choices to an LSAT question, probability theory predicts that you will guess correctly on one out of every five attempts. Of course, your chances will be greatly improved if you can eliminate one or more answer choices, and the multiple-choice nature of the test gives you the opportunity to do so.

Finally, exercise caution in handling the answer sheet. The test materials consist of a booklet containing the questions and a separate answer sheet. You indicate your responses on the answer sheet by darkening a lettered space. Be sure to code your responses completely, darkly, and neatly, and be sure that you are coding the appropriate space.

Coding out of sequence is a serious error of answer-sheet management. An error of sequence will occur if you skip a question in the test booklet but fail to skip the corresponding space on the answer sheet, or vice versa. Most examinees code answers one-by-one, but each entry requires paper shuffling. It is more efficient to code your answers in groups. Wait until you have solved five or six problems, and then enter your responses to those items on the answer sheet. Coding in groups cuts down on the paper shuffling, and it also reduces the chance of a sequence error. You will find convenient points at which to stop to perform this bookkeeping chore, e.g., as you are ready to turn a page of the test booklet. As time in a section winds down, though, start coding responses one-by-one. You do not want to run out of time before you have had a chance to code all of your responses.

ANALYTICAL REASONING

Analytical Reasoning questions can be described briefly as logical puzzles or games. Each group of questions is based on a series of statements that describe a situation such as seven children standing in a line at a movie theater, a host arranging a table seating for eight people, or a group of nine travelers to be divided into three tour groups. The questions ask about conclusions that can be deduced logically from the initial statement of the situation. Example:

> A group of six children—Mary, Frank, Ed, Dan, Sue, and Linda—took a series of tests. No two students received the same score on any given test.
> Sue scored the highest on every test.
> Mary scored higher than Frank on every test.
> Ed scored higher than Dan on every test.
> Linda's score on every test was somewhere between those of Dan and Frank.

1. Which of the following is a possible order, from highest to lowest, of student scores on a test?
   (A) Sue, Frank, Mary, Linda, Ed, Dan
   (B) Sue, Mary, Frank, Linda, Dan, Ed
   (C) Sue, Mary, Linda, Frank, Ed, Dan
   (D) Sue, Mary, Dan Linda, Frank, Ed
   (E) Sue, Mary, Ed, Dan, Linda, Frank

2. Which of the following CANNOT be the order of student scores, from highest to lowest?
   (A) Sue, Mary, Frank, Linda, Ed, Dan
   (B) Sue, Mary, Ed, Frank, Linda, Dan
   (C) Sue, Mary, Ed, Linda, Frank, Dan
   (D) Sue, Ed, Dan, Linda, Mary, Frank
   (E) Sue, Ed, Mary, Frank, Linda, Dan

3. If Mary received the third highest score on a test, then which of the following must be true of that test?
   (A) Dan received the second highest score.
   (B) Frank received the second highest score.
   (C) Dan received the fourth highest score.
   (D) Linda received the fifth highest score.
   (E) Frank received the sixth highest score.

4. If Ed received the fourth highest score on a test, then all of the following must be true EXCEPT:
   (A) Mary received the second highest score.
   (B) Frank received the third highest score.
   (C) Dan received the fifth highest score.
   (D) Ed received a higher score than Dan.
   (E) Linda received a lower score than Frank.

The first thing you will notice is that the rank ordering of the students (except for Sue) can change from test to test, that is, the information does not determine a single, unique rank ordering. This is a very important design feature of this type of question. This flexibility or open-endedness allows the test writer to ask a series of questions, each of which is related to the initial situation but is different enough from the other questions in the group to require an independent solution.

You will notice that the third and fourth questions ask you to make additional assumptions about the situation. Additional information that is provided in the form of a stipulation is to be used only in answering that particular question.

Finally, you should note that the correct answer to each question is determined entirely by deductive logic. Ignoring for the moment whether or not the questions stipulate additional information, the four questions and their correct answers have the following general forms:

1. Which of the following could be true?

    The correct answer to this form is a possible arrangement of the individuals in the problem set. The wrong answers are logically inconsistent with one or more of the rules governing the problem set.

    The correct answer to the first question is (E). (A) is wrong because Mary always scores higher than Frank. (B) is incorrect because Ed always scores higher than Dan. (C) can be eliminated because Linda's score must be somewhere between those of Frank and Dan. (D) is incorrect because Ed always scores higher than Dan. (E) is the only order that is consistent with every condition governing the problem set.

2. Which of the following cannot be true?

    The correct answer to this form is logically inconsistent with one or more of the rules governing the problem set. The wrong answers are possible arrangements of the individuals in the problem set.

    The correct answer to the second question is (C), and this question is essentially the mirror image of the first. The "CANNOT" turns the question inside-out. Four of the choices contain orders that are possible—and are for that reason incorrect choices. (C) is inconsistent with the rules governing the problem set because Linda's score must be between Frank's score and Dan's score.

3. Which of the following must be true?

    The wrong answers to a question like this are either: (a) inconsistent with the rules governing the problem set, or (b) logically possible but not logically required. The correct answer is logically deducible from the rules governing the problem set.

    The correct answer to the third question is (D). If Mary received the third highest score, then Frank scored fourth, fifth, or sixth. But Linda must have scored between Frank and Dan. So Linda must be ranked fifth with Frank and Dan ranked fourth and sixth, though not necessarily in that order. Finally, Ed must have received the second highest score, so there are two possible orders:

1. Sue	1. Sue
2. Ed	2. Ed
3. Mary	3. Mary
4. Frank	4. Dan
5. Linda	5. Linda
6. Dan	6. Frank

Thus, (D) is proved to be correct. (A) and (B) are contradicted by the diagram—they cannot possibly be true. (C) and (E) are possible orders, but they are not *necessarily* true.

4. All of the following must be true EXCEPT:

The wrong answers to a question of this form are logically deducible from the rules governing the problem set. The correct answer is either: (a) logically inconsistent with the rules, or (b) logically possible but not required by the rules. (In which case, it is not *necessarily* true.)

The correct answer to the fourth question is (C), and it is the mirror image of Question 3. With Ed receiving the fourth highest score, Dan must rank either fifth or sixth. But Linda must be between Frank and Dan with Mary higher than Frank. So Linda must be fifth, with Dan sixth, Frank third, and Mary second:

1. Sue   2. Mary   3. Frank   4. Ed   5. Linda   6. Dan

Most Analytical Reasoning problem sets use situations that we are likely to encounter in daily life: people standing in a line, a traveler planning an itinerary, a teacher selecting a committee of students. Common situations are easy to explain and so work well in the context of the LSAT. One of the common situations is the rank ordering we just discussed. You can easily imagine the possibility of other ordering problems:

Six runners—Paul, Jack, Bob, Ned, Frank, and Al—run a series of races.

A musical scale includes six notes—J, K, L, M, N, and O—that are arranged one above the other.

Before the start of a tournament, six tennis players—Jimmy, Ivan, Boris, Andre, John, and Stefan—are ranked one above the other.

Spatial Arrangements

Another common situation used by the LSAT is a spatial arrangement. Some problem sets use linear arrangements:

> *Seven children—P, Q, R, S, T, U, and V—are standing in a single-file line.*
>
> *Twelve beads—two red, three orange, two blue, two green, two black, and one yellow—are to be strung side by side.*

Other spatial arrangements are not linear:

> *Six executives—Allen, Betty, Carol, Dan, Edna, and Fred— are to be seated around a circular conference table. Six chairs are evenly spaced around the table so that each chair is directly opposite another chair. Each chair will be occupied by one executive.*
>
> *Allen cannot sit next to Betty.*
> *Carol cannot sit next to Dan.*
> *Edna must sit next to Dan.*

1. If Betty is seated next to Edna, then which of the following could be true?
   I.   Carol sits directly opposite Betty.
   II. Allen sits directly opposite Dan.
   III. Fred sits directly opposite Edna.
   (A) I only
   (B) III only
   (C) I and II only
   (D) I and III only
   (E) II and III only

2. If Allen sits directly opposite Edna, then all of the following must be true EXCEPT:
   (A) Edna sits next to Betty.
   (B) Dan sits next to Fred.
   (C) Betty sits next to Carol.
   (D) Carol sits directly opposite Dan.
   (E) Fred sits directly opposite Carol.

1. **(B)** Given that Betty sits next to Edna and Edna next to Dan, we have two possible arrangements for those three executives:

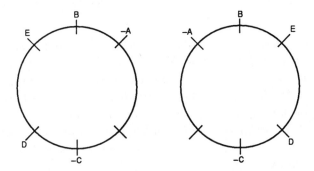

The diagrams show that only statement III can be true.

2. **(E)** The stipulation given in the question stem creates one of two seating arrangements:

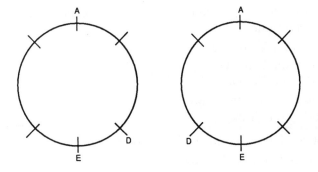

Since Allen does not sit next to Betty and since Carol does not sit next to Dan, we have only two possible arrangements:

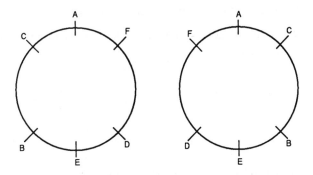

Thus, choices (A) through (D) are necessarily true while (E) is necessarily false.

Scheduling Set

Another common situation is the temporal ordering or scheduling situation:

A casting director is scheduling auditions during a certain week for seven performers: M, N, O, P, Q, R, and S. There are exactly nine audition times open: one on Monday, three on Tuesday, one on Wednesday, two on Thursday, and two on Friday. Each performer will be given exactly one audition time.

Exactly two performers must audition on Thursday, and at least one performer must audition on each of the other days during the week.

N and Q must audition on the same day.

M must audition on Monday.

O cannot audition on Friday.

S must audition on Thursday.

1. Which of the following is NOT an acceptable schedule for the two auditions mentioned?
   (A) R and S on Thursday
   (B) S and P on Thursday
   (C) S and O on Thursday
   (D) O and P on Wednesday
   (E) N and Q on Friday

2. Which of the following must be true of the audition schedule?
   (A) R is scheduled for Tuesday.
   (B) O is scheduled for Tuesday.
   (C) P is scheduled for Thursday.
   (D) N and Q are scheduled for Tuesday.
   (E) Three days have exactly one audition scheduled.

3. If N and Q are scheduled for Tuesday, exactly how many different schedules are possible?
   (A) 1
   (B) 2
   (C) 3
   (D) 4
   (E) 5

1. **(D)** No additional information is provided by this question stem, so the answer can be obtained by comparing each choice to the initial requirements. The condition that requires a certain distribution of

auditions over the days of the week is very important. (D) is not an acceptable schedule since it is not possible to schedule more than one appointment on Wednesday.

2. **(E)** The initial conditions require that there be at least one audition each day of the week, so that requirement uses up five auditions. Two performers will audition on Thursday, so we have used up six auditions. Only one audition remains to be scheduled, and that audition cannot occur on Thursday. Since the seventh audition must occur on a day other than Thursday, exactly two days will have two auditions and the other three days will have exactly one.

3. **(D)** Here you will probably want to use a diagram to keep track of the information:

Mon.	Tu.	Wed.	Th.	Fri.
M	N,Q		S	−O

We know another audition is scheduled for Thursday, and that an audition is scheduled for Wednesday and another for Friday:

	Mon.	Tu.	Wed.	Th.	Fri.
	M	N,Q		S	−O
(1)			O	P	R
(2)			O	R	P
(3)			P	O	R
(4)			R	O	P

So there are exactly four possible schedules.

Selection Situations

Another important problem type is a selection situation:

The coach of a soccer team is selecting players for the team. The candidates are Joan, Karla, Lisa, Myrna, Nan, and Opal.
Lisa must be selected for the team.
Joan can be selected for the team only if Karla is also selected.
Myrna and Nan can be selected for the team only if the other is also selected.
If Karla is selected for the team, then Nan cannot be selected for the team.
If Lisa is selected for the team, then Opal must also be selected.

1. Which of the following must be true?
   (A) Myrna is selected for the team.
   (B) Nan is selected for the team.
   (C) Nan is not selected for the team.
   (D) If Joan is selected for the team, then Nan is not selected.
   (E) If Karla is selected for the team, then Nan is also selected.

2. If Joan is selected for the team, which of the following is a complete and accurate listing of the other candidates who must also be selected?
   (A) Karla
   (B) Karla and Lisa
   (C) Karla, Lisa, and Opal
   (D) Karla, Lisa, Opal, and Myrna
   (E) Karla, Lisa, Opal, Myrna, and Nan

3. If Myrna is selected to be on the team, which of the following statements is true?
   I.   Joan is not selected for the team.
   II. Karla is not selected for the team.
   III. Neither Joan nor Karla is selected for the team.
   (A) I only
   (B) II only
   (C) III only
   (D) I and II only
   (E) I, II, and III

4. If Nan is not selected for the team, then which of the following is a complete and accurate listing of the candidates who could be selected?
   (A) Lisa
   (B) Lisa and Opal
   (C) Lisa, Opal, and Myrna
   (D) Lisa, Opal, and Joan
   (E) Lisa, Opal, Joan, and Karla

   With a problem set like this, you can summarize the information using capital letters to indicate the named individuals and symbols to show the connections between the individuals:

   (1) *Lisa must be selected:*   L
   (2) *Joan only if Karla:* $J \rightarrow K$
   (3) *Myrna if and only if Nan:* $M = N$

(4) *If Karla, then not Nan:* $K \rightarrow -N$
(5) *If Lisa, then Opal:* $L \rightarrow O$

1. **(D)** From the information provided, we can draw only one further conclusion about the candidates who must be chosen: Using statements (1) and (5), we deduce that Opal must be chosen. (A), (B), and (C) are incorrect because they move from a hypothetical statement such as "If p, then q" to a statement such as "p" or "q." (E) directly contradicts statement (4) and must be incorrect. Finally, (D) is the correct choice:

   (2)   Joan only if Karla: $J \rightarrow K$
   (4)   If Karla, then not Nan: $K \rightarrow -N$
   Therefore:
         If Joan, then not Nan: $J \rightarrow -N$

   Notice that this statement does not assert that Nan is not chosen for the team. Rather, it asserts that *if* Joan is chosen, *then* Nan is not chosen.

2. **(C)** We have already noted that both Lisa and Opal must be chosen for the team, and that conclusion eliminates both (A) and (B). Further, using the stipulation provided in the question stem that Joan is selected, we reason as follows:

   (2)   Joan only if Karla: $J \rightarrow K$
         Joan is chosen: J
         Therefore, Karla is chosen: K
   Given that Karla is chosen, we reason:
   (4)   If Karla, then not Nan: $K \rightarrow -N$
         Karla is chosen: K
         Therefore, Nan is not chosen: $-N$

   This reasoning eliminates choice (E). Finally, statement (3) is really two assertions in one sentence:

   If Myrna, then Nan, *and* if Nan, then Myrna.

   Focusing on the first half of the statement, we reason:
   (3a) If Myrna, then Nan: $M \rightarrow N$
         Nan is not chosen: $-N$
         Therefore, Myrna is not chosen: $-M$

   Since Myrna is not chosen, the correct answer must be (C).

3. **(E)** All three statements are true. Since the question stem stipulates that Myrna is selected, we begin with the statement that mentions Myrna:

   (3a) If Myrna, then Nan: $M \rightarrow N$
         Myrna is selected: M
         Therefore, Nan is selected: N

Statement (4) has an equivalent form:

(4)   If Karla, then not Nan = If Nan, then not Karla.

So we reason:

(4)   If Nan, then not Karla: $N \rightarrow -K$
       Nan is selected: N
       Therefore, Karla is not selected: $-K$

So statement II is necessarily true and is part of the correct answer. Since we know that Karla is not selected, we can use the other statement that mentions Karla to draw a further conclusion. Statement (2) also has an equivalent form:

(2)   If Joan, then Karla = If not Karla, then not Joan.

And so we reason:

(2)   If not Karla, then not Joan $-K \rightarrow -J$
           Karla is not chosen: $-K$
           Joan is not chosen: $-J$

So statement I is necessarily true as well and is part of the correct response. What about statement III? We have just proved that neither Joan nor Karla is selected for the team, so statement III is necessarily true as well.

4. (E) We begin by reasoning that the list of eligible candidates includes J, K, L, M, and O. Using the stipulation provided in the question stem that Nan is not selected for the team, we use statement (3) to deduce that Myrna is not selected. The only other statement to mention either Myrna or Nan is statement (4). Although we know that Nan is not chosen, that fact does not allow us to draw any further conclusion from statement (4). Statement (4) asserts that *if* Karla is chosen, *then* Nan is not chosen. If Karla is not chosen, Nan may or may not be chosen. Since the other statements don't exclude any individuals from the team, (E) is the correct choice.

Network Situations

Another common type of analytical situation we call a network situation because a network of arrows can be used to show the relationships among the individuals in the set:

> *On a certain island live exactly six species of animals: J, K, L, M, N, and O. A zoologist has discovered the following facts about the food chain on the island:*
> *Members of J can eat only plants.*
> *Members of M and N can eat only members of J.*

Members of K and L can eat only members of M or members of N.

Members of O can eat only members of K.

1. The extinction of which of the animal species on the island would result in the extinction of every other animal species as well?
    (A) J
    (B) K
    (C) M
    (D) N
    (E) O

2. If both K and N became extinct, then which of the following species would also become extinct?
    I.   J
    II. M
    III. O
    (A) I only
    (B) III only
    (C) I and III only
    (D) II and III only
    (E) I, II, and III

We can diagram the information in the following way:

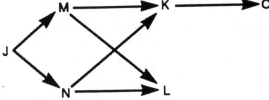

(Read "Feeds" along the arrows.)

1. **(A)** As the diagram shows, J is the first link in the entire food chain. If J is removed, then the other species are left with no food source.

2. **(B)** If K and N are removed from the chain, then O is left with no food source. L is still left with M as a food source. And J eats plants.

Organizing Table Situations

A final common type of analytical situation we call a table set because the most efficient way of attacking it is to use a table to keep track of the characteristics of a group of individuals:

Five diplomats—P, Q, R, S, and T—are attending a confer-
ence.
P speaks only English and German.
Q speaks only French, Italian, and Spanish.
R speaks only German.
S speaks only English, Italian, and Spanish.
T speaks only French and German.

1. All of the following pairs of diplomats can speak to each other
   without a translator EXCEPT:
   (A) P and R.
   (B) P and T.
   (C) Q and S.
   (D) Q and R.
   (E) R and T.

2. The language spoken by the greatest number of diplomats is:
   (A) English.
   (B) French.
   (C) German.
   (D) Italian.
   (E) Spanish.

3. If S and T wish to speak to each other, which other diplomats
   could serve as translator?
   I.   P
   II. Q
   III. R
   (A) I only
   (B) II only
   (C) III only
   (D) I and II only
   (E) I, II, and III

Here you can use an information table to keep track of the bits of
information:

	English	French	German	Italian	Spanish
P	YES	NO	YES	NO	NO
Q	NO	YES	NO	YES	YES
R	NO	NO	YES	NO	NO
S	YES	NO	NO	YES	YES
T	NO	YES	YES	NO	NO

1. **(D)** The diagram shows that Q and R do not share a common language. (A) is incorrect because P and R both speak German. (B) is wrong because P and T both speak German. (C) is incorrect because Q and S both speak Italian and Spanish. And (E) is wrong because R and T both speak German.

2. **(C)** The table shows that exactly three diplomats speak German. The other languages are spoken by only two diplomats.

3. **(D)** The table shows that S speaks English, Italian, and Spanish and that T speaks French and German. P can serve as a translator since P can speak with S in English and with T in German. Q can serve as a translator since Q can speak with S in either Italian or Spanish and with T in French. Finally, R cannot serve as a translator because R cannot speak directly with S at all.

LOGICAL REASONING

Logical Reasoning questions ask you to analyze the structure of a statement or a verbal argument and to evaluate that structure. The arguments that are the basis for Logical Reasoning questions are fairly brief, usually no more than a single paragraph. The question stem will tell you what to do with the argument; for example, attack it, defend it, or describe it. You will select an answer choice in light of the instruction given to the question stem. For example:

There is something irrational about our system of laws. The criminal law punishes a person who attempts to commit a crime even though the intended crime is never actually committed. But under the civil law a person who attempts to defraud a victim and is unsuccessful is not required to pay damages.

1. Which of the following, if true, would most weaken the argument above?
   (A) Most persons who are imprisoned for crimes will commit another crime if they are ever released from prison.
   (B) A person is morally culpable for evil thoughts as well as for evil deeds.
   (C) There are more criminal laws on the books than there are civil laws.
   (D) A criminal trial is considerably more costly to the state than a civil trial.
   (E) The goal of the criminal law is to punish the criminal, but the goal of the civil law is to compensate the victim.

The correct answer is (E). The author argues that there is a seeming contradiction in our body of laws: Sometimes a person must pay for attempted misdeeds and other times does not have to pay for attempted misdeeds. The question stem instructs us to attack the argument, that is, to find an important weakness in the structure of the reasoning. The argument asserts, in essence, that there is an inconsistency in treating attempted criminal wrongs differently from attempted civil wrongs, but if a good reason for this difference could be found, then the seeming inconsistency would disappear. This is just what choice (E) does. It points out that the law treats the two situations differently because the criminal law and the civil law aim at different goals.

The Importance of Careful Reading

Although the name of this section is Logical Reasoning, the problems are as much a test of your ability to read carefully as a test of your ability to reason logically. To do well in this section, you must read more carefully than you do when you read a textbook, a novel, a newspaper, a magazine, or other similar material. For example:

> *Three out of four clients surveyed stated that they believe that Hometown Tax Preparation Service obtained larger tax refunds for them than they would have received if they had prepared their returns themselves. Get the maximum refund you're entitled to. Let Hometown prepare and file your tax return.*

2. If the statements above are true, which of the following conclusions can be most reliably drawn from the advertisement?
   (A) Seventy-five percent of Hometown's clients believe that Hometown helped them get larger tax refunds than they would have gotten by preparing their returns themselves.
   (B) For most of its clients, Hometown is successful in helping them get larger tax refunds than they would have gotten had they prepared their own returns.
   (C) The additional tax refund obtained by using Hometown's services more than offsets the cost of paying Hometown to prepare the return.
   (D) Taxpayers who file their own returns generally do not receive the maximum refund to which they are legally entitled.
   (E) Some of Hometown's clients believe that Hometown obtained larger tax refunds for them than they could have gotten by filing their returns themselves.

The correct answer to this question is (E), and you must read the initial paragraph carefully in order to answer correctly. In the first place, you should note that the advertisement specifically says that those surveyed stated that they *believe* that Hometown helped them get larger refunds. We would not want to infer from that statement that Hometown actually did help them get larger refunds. So (B) cannot be reliably inferred from the initial statements. Next, the advertisement indicates that a survey was taken. How many people were surveyed? A hundred, as few as eight, only four? How were the people to be surveyed chosen? How many surveys had to be conducted before the company finally got the result it wanted? Since we are told nothing about the methods used to conduct the survey, we would not want to conclude anything about the client population as a whole. So (A) cannot be reliably inferred. Notice also that the advertisement does not quantify the difference between the amount of the tax refund when the return is filed by Hometown versus the amount of the tax refund when the return is filed by the taxpayer. So (C) cannot be inferred. And since the advertisement speaks only of Hometown clients, we would not want to draw any conclusion about taxpayers in general. So (D) cannot be inferred. Although the advertisement is set up to encourage the listener to conclude that Hometown actually helps people get larger refunds, the only conclusion that can really be drawn is that some of Hometown's clients believe that Hometown was successful in helping them get a larger refund. And that is choice (E).

Our advice regarding careful reading must be applied to the answer choices as well. Glance back at the problem we just studied, and compare the amount of ink used to print the answer choices to the amount of ink used to print the initial paragraph. The answer choices actually contain more words than the initial paragraph.

The Logical Structure of Arguments

When we think of logical reasoning, we often think of "pure" logical arguments such as:

(1) All persons are mortal.

(2) Socrates is a person.

(3) Therefore, Socrates is mortal.

This argument consists of three parts: a conclusion, premises, and an inference. Statement (3) is the conclusion, and statements (1) and (2) are the evidence for the conclusion. We also refer to (1) and (2) as the premises or the assumptions of the argument. The third element of the argument is the connection between the assumptions (evidence) and the conclusion. This connection is often called the inference. The inference is not found in writing. Rather, the inference is the "logic" of the argument, that is, the movement of thought from the assumptions to the conclusion. In this case, we can see that the conclusion definitely follows from the assumptions.

Few of the arguments we use in our daily lives have such a simple and tidy structure, and our conclusions rarely follow with logical certainty. We are more likely to reason:

> *The Mayor and the City Council have spent the last four weeks trying to hammer out a budget for next year. The Mayor keeps saying that city services have already been cut to the bare minimum, and the Council keeps insisting that taxes cannot be raised any further. Therefore, the city budget cannot be balanced without an increase in state aid.*

The conclusion of this argument is signaled by the "therefore." But this conclusion is not true as a matter of logic. Many things could happen to make it false that the budget cannot be balanced with an increase in state aid. The Mayor might find a way to save more money; the Council might decide to raise taxes after all; the City might find additional sources of funding such as new taxes or bonds.

Regarding arguments of the first type (the Socrates argument), we can say they are valid (logical) or invalid (illogical). We cannot use the same pair of terms to describe arguments of the second type (the City budget). Instead, we describe arguments of the second type as either weak or strong because the conclusion doesn't follow from the premises with certainty.

Analyzing an Argument

When you are asked to analyze an argument, follow these steps:

1. Locate the conclusion.

2. Carefully define the claim made.

3. Examine the connection between the premises (the evidence) and the conclusion.

The first step is to find the conclusion. Sometimes the conclusion will be the last sentence of the paragraph and will be signaled by words such as "therefore," "hence," "so," or "it follows that." If the conclusion is not so signaled you must read the argument and consciously ask, "What is the speaker trying to prove?" For example:

> *A new restaurant will open soon on the corner of Bleeker Street and Seventh Avenue, and the owners have applied for a license to operate a sidewalk café. This application should be rejected. Pedestrian traffic on that corner is heavy, particularly on Friday and Saturday nights. Moreover, that stretch of sidewalk is narrow due to the angle of intersection of the streets. A sidewalk café would seriously obstruct pedestrian traffic, causing inconvenience and even creating a safety hazard as pedestrians are diverted into the street.*

3. Which of the following best expresses the conclusion of the argument above?
    (A) A new restaurant should not be permitted at the intersection.
    (B) The new restaurant should not be permitted to operate a sidewalk café.
    (C) A sidewalk café at the location of the new restaurant would pose a danger to pedestrians.
    (D) Pedestrian traffic at the intersection is heaviest on Friday and Saturday nights.
    (E) The angle at which the streets intersect makes the sidewalk narrow.

This question asks us to locate the conclusion of the argument. The conclusion of the argument is not conveniently signaled for us, so we must ask of each idea whether it is the conclusion of the argument. For example, is the speaker trying to prove that a new restaurant will soon open at the intersection? No, so that idea is one of the premises and not the conclusion. What the speaker is ultimately hoping to prove is that the application should be rejected, so the conclusion of this argument is found in the second sentence. Thus, the correct answer is (B).

As for step two, once you have located the conclusion of the argument, make sure that you understand exactly what is claimed. First, speakers are entitled to delimit their claims quantitatively by using words such as "some," "all," "none," "never," "always," "usually," "sometimes," and "probably." And you don't score debating points by attacking a claim your opponent hasn't really made:

John: *We learned in biology today that most mammals live on land.*

Fred: *That's not true. Just the other day the teacher said that whales are mammals that live in the sea.*

4. Fred's remarks show that he has misunderstood John to say that:

(A) some mammals do not live on land.
(B) no mammals live on land.
(C) all mammals live on land.
(D) all animals that live in the sea are mammals.
(E) whales are not true mammals.

As the question stem indicates, Fred has misunderstood John and has attacked a claim that John hasn't made. Fred's response would be appropriate had John said "All mammals live on land." Only then would Fred's exception have made a valid point. So the correct answer to the problem is (C).

Additionally, speakers carefully define their claims by using descriptive words and phrases. It is simply impossible to give an exhaustive list of the ways in which arguments are delimited by descriptive words and phrases, but an example should put you on the right track:

In nations that have a bicameral legislature, the speed with which legislation is passed is largely a function of the strength of executive leadership.

Notice here that the speaker makes a claim about "nations," so (at least without further information) it would be wrong to apply the author's reasoning to states (such as New York), which also have bicameral legislatures. Further, we would not want to conclude that the author believes that bicameral legislatures pass different laws from those passed by unicameral legislatures. The author mentions only the "speed" with which the laws are passed—not their content. And since the claim covers only "legislation," we are not entitled to draw any conclusion about executive or judicial action.

At step three you evaluate the inference of the argument, that is, you ask whether or not the evidence really does support the conclusion. Often an argument used by the LSAT will be weak because the conclusion rests on some unstated premise. Examine the following line of reasoning:

This animal has eight legs.
Therefore, this animal is a spider.

The conclusion of this little argument is readily identifiable and easily understood, but does the evidence provide complete support for the conclusion? No. The conclusion follows from the evidence or single premise only on the further assumption that spiders are the only animals with eight legs:

Only spiders have eight legs.
This animal has eight legs.
Therefore, this animal is a spider.

Now the conclusion does follow logically from the evidence. The argument as originally presented depended upon a hidden or unstated premise.

There is nothing unusual in this. Most of the arguments we make are incomplete in one way or another. You might say, for example, to a dinner guest, "Pamela is not answering her office phone, so she is on her way home." That reasoning qualifies as an argument:

Pamela is not answering her office phone.
Therefore, she is on her way home.

But the conclusion requires something else:

If Pamela is not answering her office phone, then she is on her way home.
Pamela is not answering her office phone.
Therefore, she is on her way home.

Supported with this additional premise, the argument is logically valid.

Some LSAT questions may ask you to identify the unstated premise of an argument:

The notion of justice is not universally shared by all people. The tribespeople of Central Amaranda have no word for justice. The closest approximation to our word justice is payyup, a word that denotes the obligation to return that which has been borrowed. Payyup has only this limited meaning, and the language contains no other word that even approximates justice.

5. The speaker's conclusion rests on which of the following unstated premises?
    (A) The tribespeople of Central Amaranda have no written language.
    (B) The language of the tribespeople of Central Amaranda is the only language without a word for justice.
    (C) Although the notion of justice is not universally shared by all people, other values are universally shared.
    (D) A concept cannot exist unless there is a single word in a language to denote that concept.
    (E) There are no other concepts for which the language of Central Amaranda lacks translational equivalents to the English language.

The correct answer to this question is (D). The first sentence of the argument contains its conclusion, and the evidence provided for the conclusion can be summarized by saying that the language studied has no single word for the concept of justice. Thus, the argument would have this structure:

> *This language has no single word for the concept of justice. Therefore, the people who speak this language have no concept of justice.*

Having rendered the argument in this way, we can see that something is missing: A concept can exist only if denoted by a single word in a language. Thus, (D) correctly isolates an idea upon which the argument depends and that is not actually stated in the paragraph.

Frequently Used Argument Types

There are some connections between conclusion and evidence that the LSAT tests frequently, and the key to these questions is often easily identified. First, some arguments are based upon analogies:

> *Some diplomats are assigned to countries where the political conditions are unstable and the risk of violent harm great. Just as the government provides combat premiums as part of the pay to soldiers in war zones, so too the government should provide some sort of combat pay to diplomats working in politically unstable regions.*

The argument relies on an analogy between diplomats and soldiers, and the comparison seems to have some merit. Of course, the analogy is not perfect—no analogy can be more than an analogy. But some analogies are clearly so imperfect that they have no persuasive force:

> People should have to be licensed before they are allowed to have children. After all, we require people who operate automobiles to be licensed.

In this case, the two situations—driving and having children—are fairly dissimilar, and the argument is weak.

When analyzing an argument based on analogy, focus on the most important dissimilarity between the situations being compared. In all likelihood, the biggest difference will be the key to the problem:

> Something must be done about the rising cost of our state prisons. It now costs an average of $225 per day to maintain a prisoner in a double-occupancy cell in a state prison. Yet, in the most expensive cities in the world, you can find rooms in the finest hotels that rent for less than $200 per night.

6. Which of the following, if true, would be the most serious objection to the argument?
   (A) Many prisoners would prefer to be housed in single-occupancy rather than double-occupancy cells.
   (B) The most expensive hotels in the world have rooms that cost more than $200 per night.
   (C) The cost of maintaining a prison includes costs such as security and meals that hotels do not incur.
   (D) Many prisons are not located in the center of large cities.
   (E) A hotel guest is permitted to choose a hotel, while a prisoner is assigned to a particular institution.

Although prisons and hotels both house people, there are important differences between the two, e.g., prisoners are kept for long periods of time and must be fed and kept from leaving. This difference is the key to the problem; and if you study the answer choices, you will see that (C) correctly identifies the weakness in the analogy.

A second type of reasoning often seen on the LSAT is causal reasoning. Questions often ask that you evaluate the strength of an argument of the following sort:

   A recent survey by the Department of Labor revealed that
increases in the salaries of ministers are accompanied by
increases in the average consumption of rum. From 1985 to
1990, salaries of ministers increased on the average 15 percent
and rum sales grew by 14.5 percent. From 1980 to 1985, the
average salary for ministers rose by only 8 percent, and rum
sales grew by only 8 percent. This demonstrates that higher sal-
aries for ministers cause an increase in the consumption of
rum.

The causal connection asserted by the argument is very doubtful.
Although the statistics may be accurate, there is probably some other
causal explanation such as:

   Increases in ministers' salaries are the result of general eco-
nomic conditions, and these general economic conditions also
have an effect on the sale of liquor. So rather than increased rum
consumption being caused by increased clergy salaries, both are
the effects of some third factor.

When you evaluate an argument of this sort, ask yourself whether
there could be an alternative causal explanation for the phenomenon
cited:

   At the beginning of 1990, the Town of Lake George imposed a
"bed" tax on all hotel bills equal to two percent of the amount of
the bill. The summer of 1990 was the worst year for tourism in
Lake George in a decade. On January 1, 1991, the Town
repealed the "bed" tax, and tourism for the summer of 1991 was
up 20 percent over the previous year. We can see now what a
devastating economic impact the "bed" tax had on the Lake
George tourism industry.

7. Each of the following indicates a possible flaw in the reasoning in
   the passage above EXCEPT:
   (A) The nation was in a recession in 1990 but had recovered by the
       summer of 1991.
   (B) From 1990 to 1991, hotels in Lake George reduced their room
       rates by an average of 15 percent.
   (C) Over the first six months of 1991, the Lake George Commis-
       sion on Tourism heavily advertised the community as a vaca-
       tion spot.

(D) For Bolton Landing, the town next to Lake George with no "bed" tax in 1990, the summer of 1990 was the best for tourism in the town's history.

(E) Fun Park, a major tourist attraction in Lake George, was closed the entire summer of 1990 for renovation.

The initial paragraph contains a causal explanation. To answer the question we must try to anticipate possible alternative explanations for the poor summer of 1990. (A), (B), (C), and (E) all provide alternative explanations, so the correct answer is (D). In fact, (D) tends to strengthen the speaker's argument by suggesting that the "bed" tax did prompt tourists to avoid Lake George in favor of Bolton Landing.

A third type of reasoning that often appears on the LSAT is generalization:

> Kim is the first person from the South I have ever met, and she is very polite. So all Southerners must be polite.

> Every time I have visited the museum, it has been mobbed with people. Therefore, the museum must always be filled with people.

Each of these arguments use a sample experience to support a broader conclusion about the world. And in each case, the strength of the argument depends upon the representativeness of the sample experience. When you are asked to attack a generalization on the LSAT, the correct answer will probably point out that the sample is not representative:

> It is sometimes argued that we are reaching the limits of the earth's capacity to supply our energy needs with fossil fuel. In the past ten years, however, as a result of technological progress making it possible to extract resources from even marginal wells and mines, yields from oil and coal fields have increased tremendously. There is no reason to believe that there is a limit to the earth's capacity to supply our conventional energy needs.

8. Which of the following statements most directly contradicts the conclusion drawn above?

(A) Even if we exhaust our supplies of fossil fuel, the earth can still be mined for uranium.

(B) The technology needed to extract fossil fuels is very expensive.
(C) Even given the improvements in technology, oil and coal are not renewable resources, so we will exhaust our supplies.
(D) Most of the land under which marginal oil and coal supplies lie is more suitable to cultivation or pasturing than to production of fossil fuels.
(E) The fuels that are yielded by marginal sources tend to be high in sulphur and other undesirable elements that aggravate the air pollution problem.

This line of reasoning is a little like saying "Every day last week I was able to squeeze a little more toothpaste out of that flat tube by mashing it a little harder, so the tube contains limitless toothpaste." We should not assume that we can continue to squeeze harder and harder to get more fossil fuel. One day, the tube will be empty—as (C) points out.

READING COMPREHENSION

On the LSAT, reading comprehension questions are based on selections of about 550 to 600 words, with each selection supporting between six and eight questions. The 35-minute section will contain four selections and have a total of 26 to 28 questions.

The first point that should be made with regard to reading comprehension is that you should not expect to be familiar with the topics discussed in the reading selection. In fact, the test writers go out of their way to find material that most test-takers will not have seen before in order to avoid giving anyone an unfair advantage. Should you encounter material with which you are already familiar, consider that a bonus; but do not expect that you will. Reading comprehension is designed to test reading skills, not substantive knowledge.

Second, reading comprehension passages have the annoying feature that they seemingly begin in the middle of nowhere. Imagine starting to work on a selection that begins with the following sentence:

The basis of mutual understanding that, at the roots of the natural sciences is presupposed by participants in the processes of inquiry, is claimed by the cultural sciences as their authentic realm.

Your reaction is likely to be "What?" In fact, the passage in which this sentence appears treats a topic with which you probably do have some familiarity: To what extent are the behavioral sciences, e.g., sociology, like the hard sciences, e.g., physics? Although you may not remember any specifics about the debate, you probably read something about it in your introductory courses in college.

What makes this sentence so jarring is that you lack a context. Think about the reading you are accustomed to doing. First, it is usually something you have selected out of interest. You pick up a newspaper or a news magazine, and you read those articles that hold for you some intrinsic interest, for example, movie reviews but not sports. Second, the material has a context. For example, newspapers and news magazines use headlines. Before you begin to read, you know what the topic is. Our isolated sentence, above, would have been much less jarring had it been preceded by a title: ARE SOCIAL SCIENCES REALLY SCIENCE? Third, even this headline would be much less startling if you found it in what you knew to be an elementary sociology text. You might even have expected it. In any event, realize that you will have to begin your reading on the LSAT without the benefit of any prior warning.

A third characteristic of the passages is their density. The prose is fairly dry and very compact, and it won't be very much fun to read. Do not, however, let this and the other features of the reading comprehension selections intimidate you. It is expected that most test-takers will have to wrestle with the text of the selection. So if you find yourself thinking "These test people must be a lot smarter than I to know all this stuff," just remember there is nothing wrong with you. The problem is created by the design of the test.

The Six Types of Reading Comprehension Questions

Although the Reading Comprehension section uses a variety of topics, every question can ultimately be classified as one of six types. In fact, the reading selections are chosen and edited for their ability to support questions of the six types:

1. Main Idea Questions

Each Reading Comprehension passage is unified by some central theme. The passage makes some main point, and main idea questions ask about this main point. They are often worded as follows:

Which of the following best describes the main point of the passage?

The primary purpose of the passage is to . . . .
The author is primarily concerned with . . . .
Which of the following titles best describes the content of the passage?

For a main idea question, select an answer choice that captures the overall development of the selection. Avoid answer choices that mention only a part of the selection or that go beyond the scope of the selection.

2. Supporting Idea Questions

These questions ask about details that are explicitly mentioned in the passage. A supporting idea is not the main idea, so this type differs from the first type discussed above. Additionally, the ideas used by the author to support the main point are explicitly mentioned. Supporting idea questions are often worded as follows:

According to the passage . . . .
The author mentions . . . .
Which of the following questions does the author answer in the passage?

The answers to supporting idea questions are to be found in the text itself. Take your cue from the question stem, and find the particular part of the selection that contains the answer to the question.

3. Implied Idea Questions

These questions are to be distinguished from supporting idea questions in that the answers to implied idea questions are not explicitly stated in the passage. Often, an author will make a point by suggestion rather than by explicit statement. These questions ask about such meaning. These questions are often phrased:

It can be inferred from the passage that . . . .
Which of the following can be inferred from the passage?
The author implies that . . . .
The author uses the phrase ". . ." to mean . . . .

4. Logical Structure Questions

As we have noted, the passage constitutes a unified whole, that is, a central thesis supported logically by explicit points. Logical structure questions ask about the way the passage is put together. They are often phrased as follows:

The development of the passage is primarily . . . .
The author develops the passage primarily by . . . .
The author cites . . . in order to . . . .
The author mentions . . . in order . . . .

5. Further Application Questions

These questions ask that you abstract from the specific content of the passage and apply the author's ideas to a new situation. The further application question may be the most difficult of the six types because it asks that you go beyond what is explicitly mentioned or even strongly implied. These questions are often phrased as follows:

With which of the following conclusions would the author be most likely to agree?
With which of the following statements would the author be least likely to agree?
Which of the following statements, if true, would most weaken the conclusion that . . . ?
Which of the following would be a logically appropriate topic for the author to take up in the next paragraph to continue this passage?

6. Attitude Questions

These questions ask that you draw some conclusion about the author's attitude toward a subject or about the author's style. You will use clues in the passages, such as adjectives used by the author, to determine whether the author is supportive, critical, disinterested, etc. These questions are often phrased as follows:

The tone of the author's closing remarks can best be described as . . . .
The tone of the passage can best be described as . . . .
The author's attitude toward . . . can best be described as . . . .

Reading Techniques

In general, we may say that Reading Comprehension requires that you *understand* and *evaluate* the passage, but there are levels of understanding and evaluation. Obviously, there are times when you need only a general understanding of what you are reading, other times when you need a more precise understanding. Sometimes you are required to be very critical of written material; on other occasions it is sufficient if you just understand it. Taking our cue from the structure of a Reading Comprehension exercise, we ask: What do you need to learn from the passage?

We identify four levels of understanding and evaluation. First, you must have an understanding of the overall idea or main point of the passage. Not only will you need this information to answer any main idea questions, you cannot hope to make sense of the details unless you understand the overall development. Second, you must have a general understanding of the content and substructure of the passage. You must read and comprehend the specific ideas and appreciate the roles they play in the overall development. Third, it may be necessary to subject some of the specific ideas to closer scrutiny, to ask, for example, exactly what the author means by or what precise role a particular piece of information plays. Fourth, there is a level of understanding and evaluation that moves beyond the explicit. At the fourth level you are asking questions such as what further conclusions might be drawn from the information.

These four levels are not completely independent of one another, and a good reader is likely to work on all four levels simultaneously. Still, there is a certain priority to the levels. You need the overall understanding of the first level to make sense of the general understanding of the second level. You need the general understanding of the second level for the very precise understanding of the third level. You need a full understanding of the overall structure, general idea, and specific details to reach conclusions on the fourth level.

These observations can help you organize your reading attack. Your attack should aim first at the overall and general understanding of the selection. Then specific questions will guide you in determining which ideas need further study. To help get the overall idea of the selection, begin your attack by previewing the first sentence of each paragraph. The first sentence of a paragraph is often the topic sentence, and reading the topic sentences of the three or four paragraphs in the selection will give you some idea of the subject and general development of the selection. Then, as you read the selection, consciously ask yourself "What is the point the author is ultimately trying to make?"

As you read each particular point in the development of the selection, consciously ask yourself "What role does this point play in the overall development of the passage?" This will help you grasp the significance of the supporting ideas introduced by the author.

If you come across material that seems too difficult to understand, read through the material and then bracket it. By that we mean don't labor overly long trying to absorb some specific detail. Try to understand the significance of the detail in the overall scheme of the passage and move on. You know where to find the material if a question makes it necessary for you to study that particular point.

You should strive to finish your initial reading of a selection in two to three minutes, and to do so you don't need speed-reading techniques. The passage is only 550 to 600 words long. So even assuming you read at the fairly relaxed rate of 200 words per minute, you'll finish your initial reading in no more than three minutes. It is important not to spend too much time reading, because you will need time to answer the questions. And remember that you can always go back to the passage to look up specific points.

Sample Reading Comprehension Passage with Questions

The spread of Christianity to Africa may be regarded as the religious aspects of Western expansion. European missionaries naturally favored the aims of their respective countries, even as they viewed the extension of Western hegemony as redemptive, insofar as it brought Africans freedom from oppression, anarchy, and the slave trade. The glory of God and the glory of country were intertwined in the missionary thought, and many missionaries saw salvation for Africa in terms of Western civilization, of which Christianity was an integral element. To the missionary, the spirit of the Christian God was history's engine; but so closely tied to specific national interests was this belief that when Catholics and Protestants competed for the same African souls, as in Uganda, it left deep social cleavages. Converts to Catholicism became known as "bafransa," after the nationality (French) of the missionaries, while Anglicans were referred to as "baingereza," the Ganda word for the English. So deep was this division that political loyalties subsequently followed the same division, a legacy that has inhibited the unification of the country to this day.

The task of bringing Western "civilization" to Africa encountered great difficulty because of what were from the standpoint of African thinking inherent contradictions: on the one hand, its secular technique is based on profound materialism; on the other, its dominant religion, Christianity, embodies values that are irreconcilable with materialism. Westerners deal with this contradiction by relegating religious experience to a separate realm, but this metaphysical discontinuity cannot be translated into African terms. In Africa, the dichotomy between ethics and behavior, between religious and social life, is unknown.

Even to those who benefited from mission school education, Christianity had only limited appeal. By insisting on a theology and a liturgy that made little sense to thoughtful Africans, the church failed to inspire the loyalty of many of those whom it had educated. Contact with the church became merely convenient—a means of enhancing one's own career prospects outside of rather than inside the institution. It is no coincidence that Kwame Nkrumah, the first President of Ghana and one of the vanguard of the Pan-African movement, advised fellow nationalist leaders to "seek first the political kingdom, and everything else will be added." When nationalist leaders like Nkrumah portrayed themselves as political Messiahs, they engaged in a counteroffensive inspired by the indigenous notion that the religious and the secular are one; and in order to dismantle colonialism, it was natural to insist on politics as supreme and hegemonic and to demand the subordination of any ideology other than that embraced by the new nationalist leadership.

Although most church leaders believed that they had no option but to follow the commands of the new political leadership, the Africanization of the church leadership encouraged the first real search for African Christianity. The objectives were to identify an African element in the field of theology and religious activities that could keep pace with the ideological strides toward greater political and cultural autonomy.

Today, a growing number of African theologians are engaged in precisely this task, often extending it to include the role of the church in society. Many Africans, however, broke away from the mission churches and started their own religious movements. In some instances, African prophets wishing to merge the Christian message with their own religious praxis were excommunicated and forced to start their own sects. As in the division and multiplication of Protestant churches in Europe in the 17th, 18th, and 19th centuries, these organizations proved particularly successful among the poor and illiterate strata of the African population. The Messianic leaders of these African sects, basing their theology on the indigenous notion that there is no such thing as a disembodied soul, significantly limited the expansion of the mission church among ordinary Africans.

We will begin with a main idea question:

1. Which of the following best summarizes the main point of the passage?
   (A) The attempt to develop an African Christianity is complicated by both the political legacy of Western expansion and Christian theology.
   (B) Western Christian missionaries to Africa sought to advance the political aims of their respective countries as well as to spread their religion.
   (C) Christianity has often been used as a political tool to help subjugate colonized people by teaching them a passive mentality.
   (D) Western Christianity can never flourish in Africa because Christian doctrines cannot be translated into the African world view.
   (E) The influence of Christianity in Africa is found primarily in the Messianic cults that attract the poor and illiterate.

The correct answer to this main idea question is (A). In the first paragraph, the author explains that Christian missionaries to Africa also had a political agenda. In the second paragraph, the author notes that the distinction drawn by Christianity between religious and political concerns is alien to African thinking. As a consequence, according to the third paragraph, those who might otherwise have become truly African Christians used the church for personal ends. According to the fourth and fifth paragraphs, attempts are now underway to develop a coherent African Christianity. (A) best describes this development.

The correct answer to a main idea question must summarize the central theme without going beyond the scope of the passage. An answer choice that fails to capture the overall development of the passage is incorrect, as (B) and (E) illustrate. (B) highlights the theme of the first paragraph, but this idea is a specific detail in the argument and not the central theme of the passage. (E) uses an idea mentioned in the final paragraph; but, again, a specific detail is not an appropriate answer to a main idea question.

On the other hand, a choice that goes beyond the scope of the passage is also incorrect, as (C) and (D) illustrate. (C) advances a very broad conclusion about the influence of Christianity; but, though the point is interesting, it is not a point made by this author in this particular passage. As for (D), the author describes the theological and political difficulties that hinder the attempt to develop an African Christianity, but the author does not say that this attempt will necessarily fail.

Next we will study an example of a specific idea question:

2. According to the passage, Western ideas were not embraced by Africans because:
   (A) Christian missionaries were overly concerned with advancing the political aims of their own countries.
   (B) early advocates of the Pan-African movement insisted that politics take precedence over religion.
   (C) the distinction between politics as worldly and religion as otherworldly is alien to Africa.
   (D) missionaries from different countries preached contradictory Christian doctrines.
   (E) the mission church failed to educate the poor and illiterate strata of the African population.

The correct answer to a specific idea question can be found in the passage, as (C), the correct answer here, illustrates. In the second paragraph, the author explains that the Western distinction between religion and politics simply did not translate into the African world view. Since the answer to a specific idea question can be found in the passage, what would make a wrong answer the least bit distracting? Wrong answers to this type of question frequently use points found in the passage, but ones that are not responsive to the question. (A), for example, is an idea mentioned in the first paragraph, but this point is not responsive to the question. Again, the other choices borrow language from the passage and are somewhat suggestive, but none is an answer to the question actually asked.

Next we take up an example of an implied idea question:

3. It can be inferred that some African religious leaders were excommunicated from the mission church because they:
   (A) refused to accept the church's teaching regarding the body-soul dichotomy.
   (B) wanted to dismantle the structure of Western colonialism.
   (C) argued that it is impossible to reconcile Christian doctrine with Western materialism.

   (D) proclaimed that politics is the supreme ideology and national-
       ism its God.
   (E) deluded the uneducated masses into thinking that their teach-
       ings were truly Christian.

   Although the answer to an implied idea question is not specifically
written in the text, neither is it very far removed from the text. The correct answer to this item is (A). In the final paragraph, the author states
that some African prophets who wanted to incorporate Christian teachings into their own religious practices were excommunicated. Still, according to that paragraph, these prophets were successful because they
appealed to the African idea that there is no such thing as a disembodied soul. Although the passage does not specifically say so, we can infer
that it was this rejection of the body-soul distinction that was the cause
for excommunication. Again, the remaining choices use language that is
suggestive, but nothing in the passage supports such conclusions.
   Here is an example of a logical structure question:

4. The author mentions the "bafransa" and "baingereza" in order to:
   (A) demonstrate that the Christian distinction between religion and
       politics is distinctly not African.
   (B) illustrate the lasting effects of the political overtones of
       Christian missionary efforts.
   (C) cast doubt on the possibility of reconciling Christian theology
       with African concepts.
   (D) draw a distinction between the religion of the educated African
       and that of the illiterate African.
   (E) preempt a possible objection to the claim that Christian mis-
       sionaries visited Africa.

   The correct answer to this item is (B). A logical structure question
asks for the *why* rather than the *what* of a particular point. In the first
paragraph, the author states that the terms "bafransa" and "baingereza"
derive from African words for French and English, respectively, and
further that the competition among those groups of missionaries left in
Uganda "deep social cleavages."
   The most difficult type of reading comprehension question is the
further application question:

5. Which of the following would be the most appropriate topic for the
   author to pursue in a paragraph following the last paragraph of the
   passage?

(A) Trace the history of the development of the Christian notion of a disembodied soul

(B) Provide further details of the attempts of the mission church to convert Africans

(C) Analyze the effects of the Pan-African movement on colonial structures

(D) Elaborate on the rise and expansion of Protestant sects in the 17th, 18th, and 19th centuries

(E) Describe attempts by contemporary theologians to reconcile Christian teachings with African concepts

The answer to this type of question is often not very satisfying. In this case, there are several directions the author might move in, and how are we supposed to know which one? If you examine the choices, you will see that four of the five would not provide continuity in the discussion, so only one of the five ideas is acceptable, and that is (E). In the last two paragraphs, the author mentions the search for an African Christianity which will presumably attempt to resolve the seeming contradictions discussed earlier in the passage.

Although (E) is perhaps not entirely satisfying, it is certainly by comparison the best suggestion. (A) is not appropriate since the author's concern is how the concept of a disembodied soul is inconsistent with African views, not how that concept developed originally. As for (B), the author's focus is on African Christianity today, not the history of the mission movement. As for (C), the author in paragraph three mentions the anti-colonial political movement, but the discussion quickly returns to the question of theology. And as for (D), the reference to Protestant sects of the 17th, 18th, and 19th centuries is merely an enlightening analogy and does not signal a change in the direction of the main theme of the passage.

Finally, here is an example of a tone or attitude question:

6. The author's treatment of the topic can best be described as:

(A) scholarly yet sympathetic.

(B) scientific yet amused.

(C) balanced yet impassioned.

(D) caustic and biased.

(E) casual and superficial.

With a question such as this, it is important to compare and contrast the judgments made by the various choices. In this case, the first words of choices (A), (B), and (C) do not seem objectionable. The passage is scholarly or scientific and does not seem unbalanced. (D) and (E), however, can be eliminated, because the passage is neutral, not caustic, and because it is serious, not casual. Next we eliminate (C). While there seems to be a hint of emotion in the author's writing, the passage can hardly be called impassioned. And we eliminate (B) because there is no suggestion of humor in the passage. (A) is the best description of the passage. While the treatment of the issues is scholarly, the author seems sympathetic to the African point of view.

THE WRITING SAMPLE

Speaking technically, the writing sample is not part of the LSAT but a separate exercise. The writing sample is not scored, but copies of your essay are sent to the law schools you have designated to receive score reports. At the test center you will be given both pen and paper for the writing sample.

From what we are able to determine, the writing sample is not a very important part of the admissions process. Although it might make a difference in a few close cases, it is basically ignored. Still, the prospect of having to write a 30-minute essay on a surprise topic can be somewhat unnerving, so we will make a couple of comments to put the writing sample in perspective. Basically, writing sample topics are both self-contained and vacuous.

First, writing sample topics are self-contained. You don't need any outside knowledge to write the essay. Consider a sample topic:

> *The Protect Our Children Foundation has received an anonymous gift of $100,000 for the construction of a sculpture in the lobby of its building. Write an argument in favor of commissioning one of two artists to do the work. Since the commission is already set at $100,000, two other considerations should guide your decision:*
>
> - *The work should attract the attention of art critics.*
> - *The work should reflect the charity's concern for children.*

> *Greg Smith is a nationally known artist whose abstract sculptures can be seen in the best museums in the country. Much of Greg's work is controversial, as he tends to be abstract and to work with unconventional materials. Greg, who was an abused child, proposes to use a combination of wood, steel, and cloth to create an abstract sculpture that suggests the pain and suffering of an abused child.*

Donna Black is a young artist who, many predict, will become one of the best-known sculptors of the next century. Her work, though not yet widely known outside of certain circles, has received much favorable commentary from art critics. Donna's style is highly representational, and she proposes a figure with open arms beckoning to small children.

Although the topic asks you to write an argument in favor of one artist over another, you don't need to know anything about art to write the argument. Everything you need—all the pros and cons—are already in the topic itself.

Second, the topic is purely vacuous. There is no right or wrong answer. There are some reasons to prefer Greg and some reasons to prefer Donna. Pick whichever artist you prefer and marshall some reasons for choosing that artist. Bring some sort of organization to the reasons, and then write your essay.

A

GUIDELINES FOR WRITING A LETTER OF APPRAISAL FOR A LAW SCHOOL APPLICANT

In this appendix, we offer some advice for people who have been asked to write a "letter of recommendation" but who do not have much experience in writing such letters.

THE PURPOSE OF YOUR LETTER

Because law schools do not usually grant interviews to candidates, they rely on third-party reports to help them get a better picture of a candidate. A specific and thoughtful letter from someone who knows a candidate well can be the factor that tips the scale in the candidate's favor.

To begin with, many law school application materials use the terms "appraisal" or "evaluation" in lieu of the traditional "recommendation." This usage reflects the desire of law school admissions officers for a detailed analysis of a candidate's abilities rather than an unsupported endorsement of the candidate's application.

PROVIDE A CONTEXT

You should begin your letter by introducing yourself. In two or three sentences, outline enough of your background so that the reader can have confidence in your judgment. You don't have to be a lawyer to evaluate the candidate's abilities, but it is important that you be able to identify and describe characteristics such as analytical ability, language skills, and personal qualities. Your brief biographical sketch must demonstrate that your experience in business, in government, in teaching, in law, or in whatever field you work has trained you to identify the characteristics mentioned.

Next, in two or three sentences, describe your relationship to the candidate. Your purpose is to make it clear to the reader that you know the candidate well enough to offer an expert opinion on the candidate's abilities. Be sure to mention how long you have known the candidate and to say enough about the circumstances that connect you to the candidate so that a reader not familiar with those circumstances will understand that you are able to evaluate the candidate's abilities.

QUANTIFY YOUR GENERAL CLAIMS

The rest of the letter will be devoted to your analysis of the candidate's abilities. It is quite natural to want to write some general conclusions about the candidate's work, but general conclusions, no matter how favorable, may not be of much use to a law school admissions officer. Descriptions such as "very intelligent," "a top student," or "an excellent prospect" don't have much content. Such phrases leave admissions officers wondering, "How intelligent is 'very intelligent'?" "How many other students are also 'top' students?" "What does 'excellent prospect' mean?"

A more effective way of expressing the sentiment suggested by the vague expressions found in the preceding paragraph is the use of specific comparative statements such as:

Replace	With
"very intelligent"	"one of the three most intelligent people ever to work for me"
"a top student"	"one of the five best students I have seen in my teaching career"
"an excellent prospect"	"will likely perform just as well as John Smith who graduated from this college and is now attending your law school"

IDENTIFY THE CANDIDATE'S STRENGTHS

In addition to some comparative statement of the sort suggested above, a good letter of appraisal will also mention specific strengths of the candidate. Be careful that you do not just repeat information that is already available from other parts of the application. There is no need to mention the candidate's grade point average, LSAT score, major, or club affiliations. The candidate provides this information to the law schools on the application form. If you need to mention something already in the candidate's file, it must be because you plan to explain the significance of that information. You might, for example, mention that the candidate was a volunteer member of a community parks committee in order to demonstrate that the candidate enjoys doing public service, or you might mention a presentation made by the candidate at a conference in order to help support the claim that the candidate has good communications skills.

Underlying your analysis is, of course, the hope that the candidate will be accepted for admission to a law school. But it is not necessary to write a letter that describes all of the candidate's attributes in "lawyerly" terms. Even if you are not a lawyer and have only a vague idea of the attributes that would make a good lawyer, you can still write an effective letter if you mention some or all of the following general qualities:

—**Analytical Ability.** We use the phrase "analytical ability" to describe a subset of the mental skills that are generally referred to as "intelligence." Here is a list of examples of what we would call analytical ability.

Problem-solving ability. Can the candidate isolate the important details of a complex problem or situation and manipulate those factors to attain a desired result?

Reasoning by analogy. Does the candidate understand whether two situations are sufficiently similar or dissimilar to make conclusions about one situation applicable or inapplicable to the other?

Goal-oriented thinking. Can the candidate define goals and options in a complex situation and evaluate those options in light of the goals?

Mental nimbleness. Can the candidate perform mental operations quickly and under pressure? Does the candidate perform well in an adversarial situation?

Healthy scepticism. Is the candidate reluctant to accept explanations at face value? Does the candidate insist on looking beneath the surface for fundamental reasons?

—**Language Mastery.** An ability to use language is obviously important to any lawyer. Law schools would consider the following evidence of language mastery:

Precision. Does the candidate exercise great care in choosing words for their exact meanings in both written and oral communication?

Logical expression. Does the written and oral communication of the candidate show an appreciation for the logic of the language? Is the candidate careful to make certain that all communications express precisely the intended thought?

Clarity of expression. Does the candidate write and speak clearly? Are the candidate's communications grammatically correct?

Understanding. Does the candidate pay careful attention to the written and oral communications of others?

—Personal Qualities

Maturity. Does the candidate make well-considered decisions? Does the candidate possess poise and self-confidence? Does the candidate show personal initiative and industriousness?

Leadership Ability. Is the candidate able to motivate others? Does the candidate exhibit organizational ability?

Sense of Civic Responsibility. Is the candidate willing to give time for others? Does the candidate have a strong sense of moral responsibility?

Social Skills. Does the candidate work and play well with others? Does the candidate show concern for the needs and feelings of others?

To help in identifying the candidate's strengths, think about some of the important events or achievements that have shaped your opinion of the candidate. Try to understand those events and achievements in terms of the characteristics identified above.

BE SPECIFIC

As you write about the candidate's strengths, be specific. Use the events and achievements that formed your opinion of the candidate to explain and justify to the reader your conclusions regarding the candidate's abilities. Describe for the reader a particularly effective speech, a certain very successful project, or an especially notable "good deed."

As noted above, sweeping generalities may not be of great value to a law school admissions officer. Therefore, your description of the candidate's achievements that you select to illustrate your conclusions about the candidate's abilities should contain enough detail so that the admissions officer will agree with your conclusions. Study the following pairs of descriptions:

Good	Better
"gave a very effective speech at the annual sales conference"	"was given a standing ovation by the 150 sales representatives at the annual sales conference"
"was in charge of our move from Denver to St. Louis"	"located appropriate office space in St. Louis, negotiated the 10-year lease, and then supervised the moving of 54 employees and $10 million worth of office equipment"
"volunteered to help the town's Little League"	"umpired at least two evening games each week and persuaded three co-workers without children to help out as score-keepers"

SAY SOMETHING NEGATIVE

Yes, say something negative! Your letter will seem more objective and therefore more credible if you mention some minor weakness of the candidate—and we stress the word "minor." A good choice for a minor weakness is some virtue that the candidate carries to extremes. For example:

Stewart is sometimes too generous with his time, a fault that occasionally causes him to say "yes" to someone in need when for his own sake he should say "no."

Another good choice is some fault that is already being corrected:

Beth is very exacting. She expects a lot of herself, and she expects a lot of her subordinates. Over the years she has worked consistently to learn to be more tolerant of weakness and more forgiving of error.

Finally, you might want to identify a weakness that would be eliminated by law school study:

Martha is so persuasive that she sometimes overwhelms her opponents even when she is wrong. I suspect that she will learn a great deal from being pitted against others who are her match in debating skill.

MISCELLANEOUS POINTS

Although your letter should be detailed, you must remember that law school admissions officers are reading thousands of appraisal letters. Make sure that your letter contains only relevant information and that it is to the point. You should consider 1-1/2 to 2 single-spaced, typed pages to be the *maximum* length. And for many candidates, the letter should be considerably shorter.

Unless you have a special tie to a particular law school, you should be able to use the same letter for all of the schools to which the candidate is applying.

Some schools supply appraisers with a special appraisal form. Typically, the form asks the appraiser to evaluate the candidate on a scale and provides additional space for subjective comments. Such forms are self-explanatory. You should make every effort to complete the form as indicated, but you may choose to attach a copy of your appraisal letter rather than use the space set aside for comments.

APPENDIX **B**

HISTORICAL PERSPECTIVE

During the colonial and immediate post-Revolutionary period of this nation, law schools, as we know them today, simply did not exist. Only one institution dedicated solely to training lawyers survived for very long during this period, and that was the Litchfield Law School founded in 1784 by a lawyer. The Litchfield school was a proprietary or private institution that did not confer degrees upon its students. Still, during its 50 or so years of operation, the Litchfield school enrolled about 1,000 students, many of whom went on to become judges and legislators. Also during this period, some universities occasionally offered lectures in law, but these lectures did not constitute a comprehensive education in the law and so did not attract many students interested in becoming practitioners.

The primary route for admission to the bar during this time was the apprenticeship system. A person desiring to become an attorney would work as a law clerk in the office of an established practitioner. During this period of apprenticeship, the law clerk was supposed to gain a mastery of legal skills by executing a variety of tasks assigned by the employer. After an indeterminate number of years, the law clerk would be deemed sufficiently learned in the law to be examined on that knowledge. A judge or other authority would question the applicant, and if the applicant demonstrated a mastery of legal concepts, the applicant was admitted to the bar.

In reality, the apprenticeship system did not always work to the advantage of the law clerk. The quality of the training depended on the willingness of the employer to instruct and to assign meaningful jobs. But the employer had a strong economic incentive not to provide meaningful instruction and to use a clerk to perform necessary but uninteresting tasks such as copying lengthy documents. Bar associations, however, worked to maintain the exploitive clerkship system by setting standards for admission to the practice of law.

The apprenticeship system continued as the traditional means of obtaining a legal education, though the system weakened considerably during the middle of the nineteenth century. As part of the movement known as Jacksonian Democracy, state legislatures reclaimed from the private bar associations the power to set standards and to establish licensing procedures for lawyers. In the spirit of democracy, requirements for admission to the bar were so liberalized that virtually anyone of "good moral character" could gain admission to the practice of law—without demonstrating any knowledge of the law. Because a detailed knowledge of the law was no longer required, fewer people opted to study law via the exploitive clerkship method. By the 1860s only 9 out of 39 states still had a clerkship requirement.

Gradually, however, the private bar associations began to reassert their political power. In 1878, at the request of several members of the Connecticut Bar Association, a national organization for lawyers was formed: the American Bar Association. The ABA lobbied states to stiffen requirements for admission to the practice of law. Eventually, the ABA would urge that law school attendance be made a prerequisite to admission to the bar.

Harvard Law School, the oldest of existing American law schools, was established in 1817 but grew little until the appointment of U.S. Supreme Court Justice Joseph Story to its faculty in 1829. Until that time, the now venerable institution was unable to compete with the Litchfield school; and at the time of Story's appointment to the faculty, Harvard Law School had only one student. Story's drawing power was so great, however, that at the end of the following year, 30 students were enrolled, and four years later the Litchfield school ceased operations. Yale Law School is the second oldest existing law school in this country and was established in 1824. By 1870, the number of law schools had increased to 28, by 1880 to 48, by 1890 to 54, and by 1901 to 100.

Even though an extensive system of university-based law schools existed in 1900, a formal legal education was not a requirement for admission to the bar. At the First Annual Meeting of the American Association of Law Schools, the president of the association specifically disavowed any intention on the part of law schools to gain a monopoly on legal education: "There must be many avenues through which admittance to the bar may be attained, and no [one] association can pretend to control them." Thus, the mission of the university-based law school, as it was conceived by its organizers, was to train more effective lawyers by providing a better and more comprehensive education. By formalizing legal education, these schools expected to produce lawyers who would be theoreticians of the law and not mere technicians.

On the view of AALS, the ABA would be responsible for setting standards for admission to the practice of law, and the AALS would concern itself solely with the quality of the education provided by its member schools. As part of their efforts to provide a better legal education, law schools instituted new admissions requirements. (As late as 1890, only one American law school required that applicants have educational credentials that would at least qualify them for admission to college.)

Gradually, lobbying efforts of the professional associations of lawyers began to have effect. By 1920, over half the states permitted attendance at a law school to satisfy any educational requirements for admissions to the bar, though law school attendance was not yet mandatory in any state. By 1940, as a means of upgrading the qualifications of lawyers (and probably as a means of limiting the number of practitioners during the Great Depression), the majority of state legislatures were persuaded to require some law school attendance as a condition for admission to the practice of law.

About this time, the AALS began to discuss the feasibility of entrance examinations for law school applicants. In 1947, representatives from several law schools (in conjunction with the recently formed Educational Testing Service), created the Law School Admission Test Board, and in 1948 the first Law School Admission Test was administered. In 1973, the Law School Admission Test Council became the Law School Admissions Council; and in 1978, Law School Admissions Services was incorporated as the operating arm of the Law School Admissions Council.

APPENDIX C

LISTING OF ABA-ACCREDITED LAW SCHOOLS

AKRON, UNIVERSITY OF
C. Blake McDowell Law Center
Akron, OH 44325-2901
http://www.uakron.edu/law/
index.html

ALABAMA, UNIVERSITY OF
P.O. Box 870382
Tuscaloosa, AL 35487
http://www.law.ua.edu

ALBANY LAW SCHOOL
80 New Scotland Avenue
Albany, NY 12208
http://www.als.edu

AMERICAN UNIVERSITY
4801 Massachusetts Ave, NW
Washington, DC 20016
http://www.wcl.american.edu

ARIZONA STATE
UNIVERSITY
P.O. Box 877906
Tempe, AZ 85287-7906
http://www.asu.edu/law

ARIZONA, UNIVERSITY OF
James E. Rogers Law Center
P.O. Box 210176
Tucson, AZ 85721-0176
http://www.law.arizona.edu

ARKANSAS, FAYETTEVILLE,
UNIVERSITY OF
Waterman Hall
Leflar Law Center
Fayetteville, AR 72701-1201
http://law-gopher.uark.edu/arklaw

ARKANSAS, LITTLE ROCK,
UNIVERSITY OF
1201 McAlmont Street
Little Rock, AR 72202-5142
http://www.ualr.edu/~lawsch/
index.htm

BALTIMORE,
UNIVERSITY OF
1420 North Charles Street
Baltimore, MD 21201
http://www.ubalt.edu/www/law

BAYLOR UNIVERSITY
P.O. Box 97288
1400 S. 5th Street
Waco, TX 76798-7288
http://www.baylor.edu/~Law

BOSTON COLLEGE
885 Centre Street
Newton Centre, MA 02159
http://www.bc.edu/lawschool

BOSTON UNIVERSITY
765 Commonwealth Ave
Boston, MA 02215
http://www.bu.edu/LAW

BRIGHAM YOUNG
   UNIVERSITY
Provo, UT 84602
http://www.law.byu.edu

BROOKLYN LAW SCHOOL
250 Joralemon Street
Brooklyn, NY 11201
http://www.brooklaw.edu

CALIFORNIA WESTERN
   SCHOOL OF LAW
225 Cedar Street
San Diego, CA 92101-3046
http://www.cwsl.edu

CALIFORNIA-BERKELEY,
   UNIVERSITY OF
221 Boalt Hall
Berkeley, CA 94720
http://www.law.berkeley.edu

CALIFORNIA-DAVIS,
   UNIVERSITY OF
School of Law
400 Mrak Hall Drive
Davis, CA 95616-5201
http://www.kinghall.ucdavis.edu

CALIFORNIA-HASTINGS,
   UNIVERSITY OF
200 McAllister Street
San Francisco, CA 94102
http://www.uchastings.edu

CALIFORNIA-LOS ANGELES,
   UNIVERSITY OF
405 Hilgard Avenue
Los Angeles, CA 90095
http://www.law.ucla.edu

CAMPBELL UNIVERSITY
P.O. Box 158
Buies Creek, NC 27506
http://webster.campbell.edu/
culawsch

CAPITAL UNIVERSITY
303 East Broad Street
Columbus, OH 43215
http://www.law.capital.edu

CASE WESTERN RESERVE
Gund Hall
11075 East Blvd
Cleveland, OH 44106-7148
http://lawwww.cwru.edu

CATHOLIC UNIVERSITY
   OF AMERICA
Washington, DC 20064
http://www.law.cua.edu

* CHAPMAN UNIVERSITY
1240 South State College Road
Anaheim, CA 92806
http://www.chapman.edu/law/

CHICAGO, UNIVERSITY OF
1111 East 60th Street
Chicago, IL 60637
http://www.law.uchicago.edu

CINCINNATI, UNIVERSITY
   OF
P.O. Box 210040
Cincinnati, OH 45221-0040
http://www.law.uc.edu

CITY UNIVERSITY OF
   NEW YORK
65-21 Main Street
Flushing, NY 11367
http://web.law.cuny.edu

CLEVELAND STATE
  UNIVERSITY
Cleveland-Marshall College of Law
1801 Euclid Avenue
Cleveland, OH 44115-2223
http://www.law.csuohio.edu

COLORADO, UNIVERSITY OF
Campus Box 401
Boulder, CO 80309-0401
http://www.colorado.edu/law

COLUMBIA UNIVERSITY
435 West 116th Street
New York, NY 10027
http://www.columbia.edu/cu/law

CONNECTICUT, UNIVERSITY
  OF
55 Elizabeth Street
Hartford, CT 06105
http://www.law.uconn.edu

CORNELL LAW SCHOOL
Myron Taylor Hall
Ithaca, NY 14853-4901
www.law.cornell.edu/admit/
admit.htm

CREIGHTON UNIVERSITY
2500 California Plaza
Omaha, NE 68178
http://www.creighton.edu/culaw

DAYTON, UNIVERSITY OF
300 College Park Ave.
Dayton, OH 45469-2772
http://www.udayton.edu/~law

DENVER, UNIVERSITY OF
7039 East 18th Street
Denver, CO 80220
gopher://gopher.cair.du.edu/1

DEPAUL UNIVERSITY
25 East Jackson Boulevard
Chicago, IL 60604-2287
http://www.law.depaul.edu

DETROIT COLLEGE AT
  MICHIGAN STATE
368 Law College Building
East Lansing, MI 48824-1300
http://www.dcl.edu

DETROIT MERCY,
  UNIVERSITY OF
651 E. Jefferson
Detroit, MI 48226
website is currently under
construction

* DISTRICT OF COLUMBIA,
  UNIVERSITY OF
4250 Connecticut Ave., N.W.
Building 48
Washington, DC 22008

DRAKE UNIVERSITY
2507 University Avenue
Des Moines, IA 50311
http://www.drake.edu

DUKE UNIVERSITY
P.O. Box 90362
Science Drive and Toweview
Durham, NC 27708-0362
http://www.law.duke.edu

DUQUESNE UNIVERSITY
900 Locust Street
Pittsburgh, PA 15282
http://www.duq.edu/law

EMORY UNIVERSITY
Gambrell Hall
1301 Clifton Road
Atlanta, GA 30322-2770
http://www.law.emory.edu

FLORIDA STATE
  UNIVERSITY
425 W. Jefferson Street
Tallahassee, FL 32306-1601
http://www.law.fsu.edu

FLORIDA, UNIVERSITY OF
P.O. Box 117620
Gainesville, FL 32611
http://www.law.ufl.edu

FORDHAM UNIVERSITY
140 West 62nd Street
New York, NY 10023-7485
http://www.fordham.edu/law/cle/
law_main

FRANKLIN PIERCE LAW
  CENTER
2 White Street
Concord, NH 03301
http://www.fplc.edu

GEORGE MASON
  UNIVERSITY
3401 North Fairfax Drive
Arlington, VA 22201-4498
http://www.gmu.edu/depart-
ments/law

GEORGE WASHINGTON
  UNIVERSITY
2000 H Street, N.W.
Washington, DC 20052
http://www.law.gwu.edu

GEORGETOWN UNIVERSITY
600 New Jersey Avenue N.W.
Washington, DC 20001
http://www.law.georgetown.edu/
lc

GEORGIA STATE
  UNIVERSITY
P.O. Box 4037
Atlanta, GA 30302-4037
http://gsulaw.gsu.edu

GEORGIA, UNIVERSITY OF
Herty Drive
Athens, GA 30602
http://www.lawsch.uga.edu

GOLDEN GATE UNIVERSITY
536 Mission Street
San Francisco, CA 94105-2968
http://www.ggu.edu/law/

GONZAGA UNIVERSITY
P.O. Box 3528
Spokane, WA 99220-3528
http://www.law.gonzaga.edu

HAMLINE UNIVERSITY
1536 Hewitt Avenue
St. Paul, MN 55104
http://www.hamline.edu

HARVARD UNIVERSITY
Cambridge, MA 02138
http://www.law.harvard.edu

HAWAII, UNIVERSITY OF
William S. Richardson School
2515 Dole Street
Honolulu, HI 96822
gopher://gopher.hawaii.edu/11/
student/ca

HOFSTRA UNIVERSITY
121 Hofstra University
Hempstead, NY 11549-1210
http://www.hofstra.edu

HOUSTON, UNIVERSITY OF
4800 Calhoun
Entrance 19
Houston, TX 77004-6371
http://www.law.uh.edu

HOWARD UNIVERSITY
2900 Van Ness Street
Washington, DC 20008
http://www.law.howard.edu

IDAHO, UNIVERSITY OF
6th & Rayburn
Moscow, ID 83844-2321
http://www.uidaho.edu/law

ILLINOIS INSTITUTE OF
Chicago-Kent College of Law
565 West Adams Street
Chicago, IL 60661
http://www.kentlaw.edu

ILLINOIS, UNIVERSITY OF
504 East Pennsylvania Avenue
Champaign, IL 61820
http://www.law.uiuc.edu

INDIANA UNIVERSITY -
  BLOOMINGTON
211 S. Indiana Avenue
Bloomington, IN 47405
http://www.law.indiana.edu

INDIANA UNIVERSITY -
  INDIANAPOLIS
735 West New York Street
Indianapolis, IN 46202-5194
http://www.iulaw.indy.indiana.
edu

INTER AMERICAN
  UNIVERSITY OF
  PUERTO RICO
P.O. Box 70351
San Juan, PR 00936-8351
http://www.derecho.inter.edu

IOWA, UNIVERSITY OF
Melrose and Byington
Iowa City, IA 52242
http://www.uiowa.edu/~/lawcoll

JOHN MARSHALL LAW
  SCHOOL
315 S. Plymouth Ct.
Chicago, IL 60604
http://www.jmls.edu

JUDGE ADVOCATE
  GENERAL'S
600 Massie Road
Charlottesville, VA 22903
http://www.jagc.army.mil

KANSAS, UNIVERSITY OF
Green Hall
Lawrence, KS 66045
http://www.law.ukans.edu

KENTUCKY, UNIVERSITY OF
209 Law Building
Lexington, KY 40506-0048
http://www.uky.edu/law

LEWIS AND CLARK
  COLLEGE
10015 S.W. Terwilliger Blvd.
Portland, OR 97219-7799
http://lclark.edu/law/index.htm

LOUISIANA STATE
  UNIVERSITY
210 Law Center
Baton Rouge, LA 70803
http://www.lsu.edu/guests/lsulaw/
index

LOUISVILLE, UNIVERSITY
  OF
Louis D. Brandeis School of Law
Louisville, KY 40292
http://www.louisville.edu/law/

LOYOLA MARYMOUNT
919 South Albany Street
Los Angeles, CA 90015
http://www.law.lmu.edu

LOYOLA UNIVERSITY-
  CHICAGO
One East Pearson Street
Chicago, IL 60611
gopher://gopher.luc.edu/11/
loyola/colleg

LOYOLA UNIVERSITY-
NEW ORLEANS
7214 St. Charles Avenue
New Orleans, LA 70118
www.loyno.edu/SchoolofLaw

MAINE, UNIVERSITY OF
246 Deering Avenue
Portland, ME 04102
http://www.law.usm.maine.edu

MARQUETTE UNIVERSITY
Sensenbrenner Hall
P.O. Box 1881
Milwaukee, WI 53201-1881
http://www.mu.edu/dept/law

MARYLAND, UNIVERSITY
OF
500 West Baltimore Street
Baltimore, MD 21201-1786
http://www.law.umaryland.edu

MCGEORGE SCHOOL
OF LAW
University of the Pacific
5200 Fifth Avenue
Sacramento, CA 95817
http://www.mcgeorge.edu

MEMPHIS, UNIVERSITY OF
The University of Memphis
School of Law
Memphis, TN 39152-6513
http://www.people.memphis.edu/
~law

MERCER UNIVERSITY
1021 Georgia Avenue
Macon, GA 31207
http://www.mercer.edu/~law

MIAMI, UNIVERSITY OF
P.O. Box 248087
Coral Gables, FL 33124
http://www.law.miami.edu

MICHIGAN, UNIVERSITY OF
Hutchins Hall
625 South State Street
Ann Arbor, MI 48109-1215
http://www.law.umich.edu

MINNESOTA, UNIVERSITY
OF
229 19 Ave S.
Minneapolis, MN 55455
http://www.law.umn.edu/

MISSISSIPPI COLLEGE
151 East Griffith Street
Jackson, MS 39201
http://www.mc.edu

MISSISSIPPI, UNIVERSITY OF
Office of the Dean
Law Center
University, MS 38677
http://www.olemiss.edu/depts/
law_school

MISSOURI-COLUMBIA,
UNIVERSITY OF
203 Hulston Hall
University of
Columbia, MO 65211
http://www.law.missouri.edu

MISSOURI-KANSAS CITY,
UNIVERSITY OF
5100 Rockhill Road
Kansas City, MO 64110
http://www.law.umkc.edu

MONTANA, UNIVERSITY OF
Missoula, MT 59812
http://www.umt.edu/law

NEBRASKA, UNIVERSITY OF
P.O. Box 830902
Lincoln, NE 68583-0902
http://www.unl.edu/lawcoll

NEW ENGLAND SCHOOL
OF LAW
154 Stuart Street
Boston, MA 02116
http://www.nesl.edu

NEW MEXICO,
UNIVERSITY OF
1117 Stanford, N.E.
Albuquerque, NM 87131-1431
http://www.unm.edu/~unmlaw

NEW YORK LAW SCHOOL
57 Worth Street
New York, NY 10013-2960
http://www.nyls.edu

NEW YORK UNIVERSITY
40 Washington Square South
New York, NY 10012
http://www.nyu.edu/law

NORTH CAROLINA CENTRAL
1512 South Alston Avenue
Durham, NC 27707
http://www.nccu.edu/law

NORTH CAROLINA,
UNIVERSITY OF
Campus Box 3380
Van Hecke-Wettach Hall
Chapel Hill, NC 27599-3380
http://www.law.unc.edu

NORTH DAKOTA,
UNIVERSITY OF
Centennial Drive
P.O. Box 9003
Grand Forks, ND 58202
http://www.law.und.nodak.edu

NORTHEASTERN
UNIVERSITY
400 Huntington Avenue
Boston, MA 02115
http://www.slaw.neu.edu

NORTHERN ILLINOIS
UNIVERSITY
College of Law
DeKalb, IL 60115
http://www.niu.edu/claw

NORTHERN KENTUCKY
UNIVERSITY
Nunn Drive
Highland Heights, KY 41099
http://www.eku.edu/~chase

NORTHWESTERN
UNIVERSITY
357 East Chicago Avenue
Chicago, IL 60611
http://www.law1.nwu.edu/

NOTRE DAME,
UNIVERSITY OF
103 Law Building
Notre Dame, IN 46556
http://www.nd.edu/~ndlaw

NOVA SOUTHEASTERN
UNIVERSITY
3305 College Avenue
Fort Lauderdale, FL 33314-7721
http://www.nsulaw.nova.edu

OHIO NORTHERN UNIVERSITY
525 S. Main Street
Ada, OH 45810-1599
http://www.law.onu.edu

OHIO STATE UNIVERSITY
55 W. 12th Avenue
Columbus, OH 43210
http://www.acs.ohio-state.edu/
units/law

OKLAHOMA CITY
UNIVERSITY
2501 North Blackwelder
Oklahoma City, OK 73106
http://www.okcu.edu/~law/
home.htm

OKLAHOMA, UNIVERSITY
  OF
300 Timberdell Road
Norman, OK 73019-5081
http://www.law.ou.edu

OREGON, UNIVERSITY OF
1221 University of Oregon
Eugene, OR 97403-1221
http://www.law.uoregon.edu

PACE UNIVERSITY
78 North Broadway
White Plains, NY 10603
http://www.law.pace.edu

PENNSYLVANIA STATE
  UNIVERSITY
Dickinson School of Law
150 S. College Street
Carlisle, PA 17013-2899
http://www.dsl.edu

PENNSYLVANIA,
  UNIVERSITY OF
3400 Chestnut Street
Philadelphia, PA 19104-6204
http://www.law.upenn.edu

PEPPERDINE UNIVERSITY
24255 Pacific Coast Highway
Malibu, CA 90263
http://law.pepperdine.edu

PITTSBURGH, UNIVERSITY
  OF
3900 Forbes Avenue
Pittsburgh, PA 15260
http://www.law.pitt.edu

PONTIFICAL CATHOLIC
  UNIVERSITY OF P.R.
2250 Las Americas Avenue
Suite 543
Ponce, PR 00731-6382

PUERTO RICO,
  UNIVERSITY OF
P.O. Box 23349
San Juan, PR 00931-3349

QUINNIPIAC COLLEGE
275 Mount Carmel Avenue
Hamden, CT 06518-1950
http://www.quinnipiac.edu/law

REGENT UNIVERSITY
1000 Regent University Drive
Virginia Beach, VA 23464
http://www.regent.edu/acad/
schlaw

RICHMOND, UNIVERSITY OF
Law School
University of Richmond
Richmond, VA 23173
http://law.richmond.edu

ROGER WILLIAMS
  UNIVERSITY
Ten Metacom Avenue
Bristol, RI 02809
www.rwu.edu/law

RUTGERS UNIVERSITY-
  CAMDEN
217 North Fifth Street
Camden, NJ 08102-1203
http://www-camlaw.rutgers.edu

RUTGERS UNIVERSITY-
  NEWARK
15 Washington Street
Newark, NJ 07102-3192
http://www.rutgers.edu/rusln

SAMFORD UNIVERSITY
800 Lakeshore Drive
Birmingham, AL 35229
http://www.samford.edu/schools/
law

SAN DIEGO, UNIVERSITY OF
5998 Alcala Park
San Diego, CA 92110-2492
http://www.acusd.edu/~usdlaw

SAN FRANCISCO,
UNIVERSITY OF
2130 Fulton Street
San Francisco, CA 94117-1080
http://www.usfca.edu

SANTA CLARA UNIVERSITY
500 El Camino Real
Santa Clara, CA 95053
http://www.scu.edu/law

SEATTLE UNIVERSITY
950 Broadway Plaza
Tacoma, WA 98402
http://www.law.seattleu.edu

SETON HALL UNIVERSITY
One Newark Center
Newark, NJ 07102
http://www.shu.edu/law

SOUTH CAROLINA,
UNIVERSITY OF
Main and Greene Streets
Columbia, SC 29208
http://www.law.sc.edu

SOUTH DAKOTA,
UNIVERSITY OF
414 E. Clark Street
Vermillion, SD 57069-2390
http://www.usd.edu/law

SOUTH TEXAS COLLEGE
OF LAW
1303 San Jacinto
Houston, TX 77002-7000
http://www.stcl.edu

SOUTHERN CALIFORNIA,
UNIVERSITY OF
University Park
Los Angeles, CA 90089-0071
http://www.usc.edu/dept/law

SOUTHERN ILLINOIS
Lesar Law Building
Carbondale, IL 62901-6804
http://www.siu.edu/~lawsch

SOUTHERN METHODIST
UNIVERSITY
P.O. Box 750116
Dallas, TX 75275-0116
http://www.smu.edu/~law

SOUTHERN UNIVERSITY
P.O. Box 9294
Baton Rouge, LA 70813
website is currently under
construction

SOUTHWESTERN
UNIVERSITY
675 South Westmoreland Avenue
Los Angeles, CA 90005-3992
http://www.swlaw.edu

ST. JOHN'S UNIVERSITY
8000 Utopia Parkway
Jamaica, NY 11439
http://www.stjohns.edu/law

ST. LOUIS UNIVERSITY
3700 Lindell Blvd.
St. Louis, MO 63108
http://lawlib.slu.edu

ST. MARY'S UNIVERSITY
One Camino Santa Maria
San Antonio, TX 78228-8602
http://www.stmarylaw.edu

ST. THOMAS UNIVERSITY
16400 N.W. 32 Avenue
Miami, FL 33054
http://www.stu.edu/law/
lawmain.htm

STANFORD UNIVERSITY
Crown Quadrangle
Stanford, CA 94305-8610
http://www-leland.stanford.edu/
group/law

STATE UNIVERSITY OF
    NEW YORK
319 O'Brian Hall
North Campus
Buffalo, NY 14260
http://www.buffalo.edu/law/
js.html

STETSON UNIVERSITY
1401 61st Street South
St. Petersburg, FL 33707
http://www.law.stetson.edu

SUFFOLK UNIVERSITY
41 Temple Street
Boston, MA 02114-4280
http://www.suffolk.edu/law

SYRACUSE UNIVERSITY
Syracuse, NY 13244-1030
http://www.law.syr.edu

TEMPLE UNIVERSITY
1719 North Broad Street
Philadelphia, PA 19122
http://www.temple.edu/lawschool

TENNESSEE, UNIVERSITY OF
1505 W. Cumberland Ave.
Knoxville, TN 37996-1810
http://www.law.utk.edu

TEXAS AT AUSTIN,
    UNIVERSITY OF
727 E. Dean Keeton Street
Austin, TX 78705
http://www.utexas.edu/law

TEXAS SOUTHERN
    UNIVERSITY
3100 Cleburne
Houston, TX 77004-3216
http://www.tsulaw.edu

TEXAS TECH UNIVERSITY
1802 Hartford
Lubbock, TX 79409-0004
http://www.law.ttu.edu

* TEXAS WESLEYAN
    UNIVERSITY
1515 Commerce Street
Fort Worth, TX 76102
http://www.txwesleyan.edu

* THOMAS JEFFERSON
    SCHOOL OF LAW
2121 San Diego Avenue
San Diego, CA 92110
http://www.jeffersonlaw.edu

THOMAS M. COOLEY LAW
    SCHOOL
217 South Capitol Avenue
P.O. Box 13038
Lansing, MI 48901
http://www.cooley.edu

TOLEDO, UNIVERSITY OF
2801 West Bancroft
Toledo, OH 43606
http://www.utoledo.edu/law

TOURO COLLEGE
300 Nassau Road
Huntington, NY 11743
http://www.tourolaw.edu

TULANE UNIVERSITY
6329 Freret Street
New Orleans, LA 70118-6231
http://www.law.tulane.edu

TULSA, UNIVERSITY OF
3120 East Fourth Place
Tulsa, OK 74104
http://www.utulsa.edu/law

UTAH, UNIVERSITY OF
332 South 1400 East Front
Salt Lake City, UT 84112-0730
http://info.law.utah.edu

VALPARAISO UNIVERSITY
Valparaiso, IN 46383
http://www.valpo.edu/law/

VANDERBILT UNIVERSITY
21st Avenue South
Nashville, TN 37240
http://www.vanderbilt.edu/law

VERMONT LAW SCHOOL
Chelsea Street
P.O. Box 96
South Royalton, VT 05068-0096
http://www.vermontlaw.edu

VILLANOVA UNIVERSITY
299 North Spring Mill Road
Villanova, PA 19085-1682
http://www.law.vill.edu/vls

VIRGINIA, UNIVERSITY OF
580 Massie Road
Charlottesville, VA 22903-1789
http://www.law.virginia.edu/
index.htm

WAKE FOREST UNIVERSITY
P.O. Box 7206
Reynolda Station
Winston-Salem, NC 27109-7206
http://www.wfu.edu

WASHBURN UNIVERSITY
1700 College Avenue
Topeka, KS 66621
http://www.washburnlaw.wuacc.
edu/school

WASHINGTON AND LEE
   UNIVERSITY
Sydney Lewis Hall
Lexington, VA 24450-0303
http://www.wlu.edu

WASHINGTON UNIVERSITY
1 Brookings Drive
Campus Box 1120
St. Louis, MO 63130-4899
http://ls.wustl.edu

WASHINGTON, UNIVERSITY
   OF
1100 NE Campus Parkway
Seattle, WA 98105-6617
http:/www2.law.washington.edu

WAYNE STATE UNIVERSITY
468 Ferry Mall
Detroit, MI 48202
http://www.science.wayne.edu/
~law

WEST VIRGINIA
   UNIVERSITY
P.O. Box 6130
Morgantown, WV 26506-6130
gopher://wvnvm.wvnet.edu/11/
wc/wvu

WESTERN NEW ENGLAND
   COLLEGE
1215 Wilbraham Road
Springfield, MA 01119
http://www.law.wnec.edu

WHITTIER COLLEGE
3333 Harbor Boulevard
Costa Mesa, CA 92626
http://www.whittier.edu

WIDENER UNIVERSITY
4601 Concord Pike
P.O. Box 7474
Wilmington, DE 19803-0474
http://www.widener.edu/law/
law.html

WIDENER UNIVERSITY-
   HARRISBURG
3800 Vartan Way
P.O. Box 69382
Harrisburg, PA 17106-9382
http://www.widener.edu/law/
law.html

WILLAMETTE UNIVERSITY
245 Winter St. SE
Salem, OR 97301-3922
http://www.willamette.edu

WILLIAM AND MARY
   SCHOOL OF LAW
P.O. Box 8795
Williamsburg, VA 23187-8795
http://www.wm.edu/law

WILLIAM MITCHELL
   COLLEGE OF
875 Summit Avenue
St. Paul, MN 55105-3076
http://www.wmitchell.edu

WISCONSIN, UNIVERSITY OF
975 Bascom Mall
Madison, WI 53706-1399
http://www.wisc.edu

WYOMING, UNIVERSITY OF
P.O. Box 3035
Laramie, WY 82071
http://www.uwyo.edu/law/
law.htm

YALE UNIVERSITY
P.O. Box 208215
New Haven, CT 06520-8215
http://www.yale.edu/lawweb/
lawschool

YESHIVA UNIVERSITY
Benjamin N. Cardozo School
   of Law
55 Fifth Avenue
New York, NY 10003
http://www.yu.edu/csl/law

* Provisionally Approved